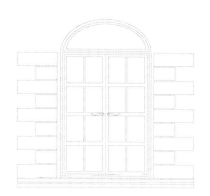

MILLSCAPE

Mansions

Homes and

Houses of

Oldham's Mill

Owners

Duncan Gurr and Tania M. C. Lewis

Dedicated to Steve, Rhys and Briony Lewis, and also to Helen Robinson.
It couldn't have done without you all.

OLDHAM
Adult and Community Services

Supported by
The National Lottery
through the Heritage Lottery Fund
Heritage Lottery Fund

Published by Oldham Arts and Heritage Publications, Publications Office, Oldham Library and Lifelong Learning Centre, PO Box 523, Greaves Street, Oldham. OL1 1AL. Copies of this book can be ordered from the Publications Office on 0161 770 8077.

ISBN 978-0-902809-92-5

MILLSCAPE
Mansions

Contents

Foreword

The majority of people will be only too aware of the whereabouts of Werneth Hall, Hathershaw Hall and Foxdenton Hall, all of which are, of course, still standing. Within the Borough of Oldham there were, at one time, many more halls and mansion houses, some larger or smaller than others, that are worthy of mention and which in many cases have long since been demolished.

With this in mind, Oldham and District Historical Society decided to produce this book. Whilst acknowledging the fact that several of the buildings have been previously researched and written about in various publications, the Society nevertheless took the view that all the information gathered should be brought together to make for easier reading and future research.

As the research gathered pace and more buildings were identified, it became obvious that only a small percentage of entries could be included in this book. The Society then had the unenviable task of trying to decide which properties to include; with the result that only around twenty of the original ninety houses have been chosen, the focus for this book being drawn towards the houses built or once occupied by Oldham's cotton mill owners. All the other entries, plus other relevant research material will eventually be made available at Oldham Local Studies and Archives, and may form the basis of future publications.

It is extremely unlikely that the pen pictures included will be fully comprehensive, or even without error. Future researchers and/or students of local and social history should therefore use this information purely as a starting point towards their continuing efforts. Photographs of some of the buildings and occupiers are included where available, as are also extracts from Ordnance Survey Maps.

I wish to place on record my thanks for the help received from Terry Berry, Roger Ivens and the staff at the Oldham Local Studies and Archives centre, the members of the Oldham and District Historical Society, and especially Sandra Ratcliff, without whose sterling work this book would have been so much more difficult to produce.

Thanks also to Keith Snape, Publications Officer, for his efforts in steering this project through to completion and Sean Baggaley, Social History Curator, Gallery Oldham, for an informative preface, contextualising the wealth of the cotton mill owners within the historic Transatlantic Slave Trade.

I sincerely hope that our efforts will be appreciated in years to come and may act as a catalyst and spur to future researchers and local historians.

Duncan Gurr
Chairman, Oldham and District Historical Society.

MILLSCAPE

4

MILLSCAPE
Mansions

Preface

This fascinating book makes a direct link between the wealth generated by Oldham's cotton mills and the substantial houses occupied by the mill owners. This minority of wealthy individuals are often overlooked these days as we concentrate on the lives of the cotton workers themselves. But take a moment to consider the very start of the production line. Where did this cotton come from?

It is now 200 years since the Transatlantic Slave Trade was abolished within the British Empire. The institution of slavery persisted until the 1830s in British colonies and later still in the cotton producing states of America. And it is these vast slave plantations that were the source of so much of Oldham's cotton. In 1860 Oldham was in receipt of nearly 8% of America's slave grown cotton crop. To express this in human terms it took over 200,000 slave workers to feed Oldham's mills that year. The best estimate would mean that for every Oldhamer working in a cotton mill there were eight slaves further down the production line. So if a mill owner employed 500 hands then his wealth also relied on 4000 slaves.

Within this book the connection between the large house and the owner's mill is sometimes very clear. Downey House, Derker Hall and Firs Hall all have an equivalent in Downey Mill, Derker Mill and Firs Mill. And in the combination of Orleans House and Orleans Mill there is even a name that makes a direct link with the American South. But where the link is not quite so obvious the authors are a great guide to the fortunes of some of the owners. There are many examples of the established wealth of families such as the Cromptons and Cleggs being invested in the early days of cotton. But alongside that are tales of new arrivals and new houses built much later as the industry matured.

The houses that do survive are to be treasured and the ones long since gone are to be mourned. Alongside the mills themselves, these houses are symbols of the great wealth generated by workers both in local mills and in distant plantations.

The Heritage Lottery Fund has contributed funding for this book and the accompanying Millscapes exhibition at Touchstones Rochdale and Gallery Oldham. It does so with the aim that previously hidden histories such as this are given greater prominence.

Sean Baggaley
Social History Curator
Gallery Oldham

Introduction

It has been said that an Englishman's house is his castle[1], implying that we who live on this beautiful isle, see ourselves not just as nation, city or town dwellers, or even in our case, Oldhamers, Saddleworthians or Roytonians (to name but a few of the areas that make up the Borough of Oldham). On a day-to-day basis we see ourselves more as lords of the area we call home. We invest immense time and effort in making our home environment a retreat from the pressures of everyday life and strive towards a level of comfort that meets our individual need. The Borough of Oldham, as we see it today, is the culmination of many people's view of their home as their castle – whether this be developers aiming to give a volume of people a home, business owners whose success has required expansion of the premises or, as in many of the cases in this book, individuals who have achieved a social standing and commissioned a dwelling that is an outward reflection of their status.

Of the latter, never was this more so in the Oldham area than in a golden age of building that was concurrent with the rise of industrialism and the growth of the cotton industry. A time when humble dwellings were expanded or extended and where new ones arose to meet the need for growing families, the migration of rural populations to urban areas and the simple desire to display ones wealth. As now, when older houses fell into disrepair or no longer met need, they were replaced with others that represented the trends, mores and expectations of the era. An era of immense change, driven in turn by scientific and artistic developments, altering our worldview and changing the lives of people at all social levels.

Oldham has been documented thoroughly and by a number of bodies, amongst the most notable being British History Online[2] and Oldham Local Studies and Archives[3]. But there is no substitute in terms of access to source material or enthusiasm for that of local historians.

The Oldham and District Historical Society has undertaken the research for this book. Over a period of many years, they have searched through numerous historical sources to uncover the hidden stories of these houses. Each source had something different to reveal and a different technique to draw out the information. Chief amongst these is the Census, cross referenced with sources such as the Burgess Roll, Street Directories and oral tradition. All of these are explained in slightly more detail in Appendices at the end of the book, for readers who may wish to extend their knowledge, to place the stories of our houses in context or simply to view the evidence for each house from an original source – a rewarding pastime. For a list of sources held by Oldham Historical Society, visit: http://www.oldham.gov.uk/community/local_studies/family-history.htm

The histories of our houses are closely bound with that of Britain's Industrial Revolution; in fact Manchester was the cradle of this huge social change, with the surrounding mill towns playing a major part. This huge topic has spawned a welter of literature and to attempt to address it in any depth here would do it a great injustice. Suffice to say, that the Internet links throughout this book will hopefully allow readers to access the topic in more depth and gain a greater understanding of the context in which this book is set.

'Castle' may be a grand way to describe the average Oldham house in days gone by, but in choosing these examples, we have tried to show a range of important homes in the Borough - not all of which still stand – but each of which take us on a journey revealing the past changes within the community which have created the Borough as we know it today. We think the journey will surprise you as you discover that the basic motivations of our ancestors were not that different to those of today. In turn, it may prompt you to consider the architectural and social legacy that we leave for the next generation of Oldhamers.

Tania M. C. Lewis

[1]"This saying is as old as the basic concepts of English common law." From the "Morris Dictionary of Word and Phrase Origins" by William and Mary Morris (HarperCollins, New York, 1977, 1988).
"You are the boss in your own house and nobody can tell you what to do there. No one can enter your home without your permission. The proverb has been traced back to 'Stage of Popish Toys' (1581). In 1644, English jurist Sir Edward Coke (1552-1634) was quoted as saying: 'For a man's house is his castle, et domus sua cuique tutissimum refugium' ('One's home is the safest refuge for all'). First attested in the United States in 'Will and Doom' (1692). In England, the word 'Englishman' often replaces man." From "Random House Dictionary of Popular Proverbs and Sayings" by Gregory Y. Titelman (Random House, New York, 1996). http://www.phrases.org.uk/bulletin_board/8/messages/1239.html
[2] 'The parish of Prestwich with Oldham,' A History of the County of Lancaster: Volume 5 (1911), pp. 67-76. URL: http://www.british-history.ac.uk/report.asp?compid=53001 (Accessed March 2007)
[3]http://www.oldham.gov.uk/community/local_studies/oldhams-archives.htm

Abbeyhills House

Abbeyhills House c. 1930.
© E. Perry. Reproduced with the kind permission of E. Perry.

If you leave Oldham Town Centre, just east of the Oldham by-pass via Park Road, towards Glodwick, you will find yourself on the eponymous Abbeyhills Road. However, most people regularly using this road probably have no idea that its name originally derived from the outstanding house located at one end of it.

Abbey Hills House (as it was once written) was originally an 18th Century farmhouse. The house was a substantial stone-built structure with a large, pleasant garden containing many healthy trees. We don't know exactly when it was built, but we do know that the house was one of the most favourably situated old homes about Oldham. But in saying that, we need to put the house into the context of the age. At a time when most workers drew their water from a communal water source, such as the village or street pump, or as frequently a free running water source such as a stream, the water at Abbeyhills House was pumped from a well in the kitchen. In addition, there was another well in the yard, which never ran dry, presumably fed from a spring from higher up in Springhead.

The house was roofed with stone flags and the original timber beams were just as when the trees were cut down to provide them. By the standards of the day, Abbeyhills House was a desirable property. There are many surviving examples of houses today with such features, but modern developments such as running water, sanitation and electricity, make them desirable as homes.

The building originally stood near to where the Manor Inn now stands. It must be remembered that Abbeyhills Road used to terminate at its junction with Manor Road and the highway, which was little more than a track, then wound its way past the Manor House at Lowside and down to Pitses, where it divided to give access to either Ashton–under-Lyne or Lees. The extension to Abbeyhills Road (B6194), which leads directly to Ashton-Under-Lyne, was not built until well into the 20th Century. The Survey Plan of 1931, which shows the position of the house, also reveals the farmland that was removed to create this road. Abbeyhills House stood in graceful solitude, in a pastoral setting and would have been approached through gates and a driveway where the shops now stand, further enhancing its status as a grand dwelling.

The 1841 Census lists the property under its original name, as Wabbow Hills, an earlier way of spelling the name, from the Middle English, 'Quabba,' meaning marsh. The occupiers are given as William Wrigley, a coal master and his wife Kitty, who were both described as being fifty years of age, although later Censuses seem to indicate that this was incorrect. It is uncertain how this discrepancy occurred and could be due to factors such as inaccurate or non-existent birth records or mistakes in recording data. This is a common occurrence with early Census data.

The Census gives us further information about the manner in which they were living. In common with other people of their social standing, the Wrigleys had two servants living in at the house. The nature of their work is not revealed, but their tasks may have ranged from general cooking and cleaning to assisting the master of the house with menial tasks and the mistress with household ones. It was not uncommon for the householder of a small estate to employ a husband and wife team to assist himself and his wife, however,

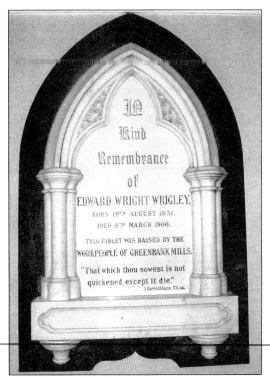

Memorial tablet to Edward Wright Wrigley, St. Mark's Church, Glodwick.
©D. Gurr. Reproduced with the kind permission of D. Gurr.

we have no evidence as to whether this was the case at Abbeyhills House.

By the time of the 1851 Census, a mere ten years later, the building was listed at Lowside, with William now described as not only a coal master but also a farmer employing four men and forty boys. This represents quite a change in circumstances and we are only left to imagine the changes this would have made to the everyday lives of the inhabitants of the then Lowside. The size of this workforce leads one to believe that most, if not all of them, were part-time scholars, living locally. We can assume that the growth of William Wrigley's business must have had an impact not only on the house, but also on the surrounding population, as jobs were created.

William and Kitty were now correctly listed as being 63 years old and also living at the property were John Wrigley, their 26-year-old unmarried son who was a cotton spinner; William Lees Evans, a surveyor's assistant, who was their 18-year-old nephew; plus two servants. Despite the growth of the household through the inclusion of a son and nephew and the number of farm workers, the number of servants remained the same.

The next Census of 1861 shows a very different picture. With William and Kitty Wrigley, the latter now referred as Kate, now in their seventies, they only employed one servant. William is now described solely as a farmer of 15 acres of land and the considerable workforce of a decade ago has dwindled to just two men. Old age had brought with it reduced circumstances and we are left to imagine what it might have been like living in such a large house, amidst the depth of farmland with the amenities of the time and a sole companion.

It is assumed that both William and Kitty Wrigley died sometime between the 1861 and 1871 Census information. By 1871, and by coincidence, another Wrigley family occupied Abbeyhills House, although they were not related: Edward Wright Wrigley, a 39-year-old master cotton spinner; his wife Mary, aged 33 years; and three sons: Arthur Edward, age 6; Harold, age 4; and Vincent Shiers, age 3; together with three servants. Wrigley was a common name in the area, as evidenced through existing examples such as the solicitor Wrigley Claydon; Wrigley Street in the Greenacres area; the house names of Wrigley at Blue Coat School; and a genealogy of the Wrigley family can be found on the Internet recording their contribution to the life of Lancashire from 1580 onwards[4].

It is at this time that we first find a record of the house being referred to as Abbeyhills Hall. We have no evidence to suggest why the name was changed and it could possibly have been a way for the second Wrigley family to make their own mark, distinguishing it from the previous Wrigleys.

Around this time the house was re-modelled with a modern brick extension to the front. Edward, who was to become one of Oldham's better-known cotton spinners, a partner in the giant Glodwick firm of Lees and Wrigley Ltd. of Greenbank Mills, had become a Justice of the Peace. We can assume, therefore, that his house was considered to be commensurate with his position as an important personage.

The family stayed at Abbeyhills until 1880 when they moved to Thornycroft House on the Coppice (see separate entry). When Edward died on March 8th 1900, aged 68 years, a stained glass window was installed to his memory in St. Mark's Church, Glodwick, by his

[4] http://genforum.genealogy.com/wrigley/

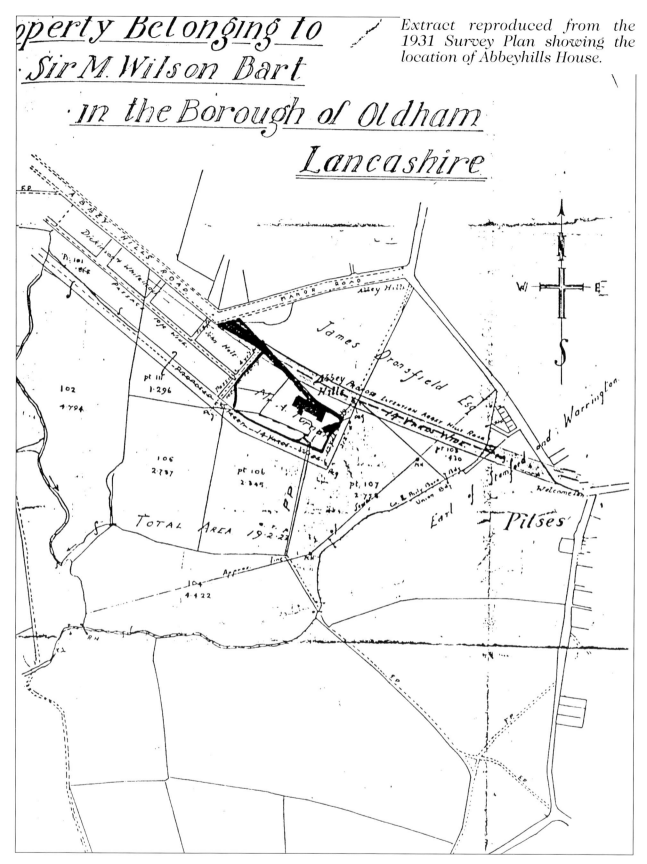

widow and sons. His workforce also erected a marble plaque there. Both the Lees and Wrigley families of Greenbank Mills were parishioners of this church and, in fact, were principle benefactors when it was built in 1876, together with its adjacent schools.

A year later, the 1881 Census reveals that the Wrigleys were succeeded at Abbeyhills House by another cotton spinner, Robinson Sinkinson of King Street Mill and his wife Betty, both described as being 42 years of age. With them the household grew; they had a total number of five sons and one daughter: Henry Herbert, aged 17, an assistant cotton spinner; Edith Annie, aged 14; Frank, 12; Percy Stanley, 11; George, 6; and Robert Francis, 5 – all of whom were scholars. We also know that they lived there until the turn of the 20th Century. Over this period of ten years or more, no documents have yet been found that give us a further indication as to the circumstances of the house. However, this was a decade of some change socially and technologically. We can assume that Abbeyhills House at the end of the 19th Century was a significantly different one from that of the 1700s.

Arthur Turner, the architect possibly best remembered for his design of the Elk Mill[5], was the next occupant and he and his wife, Edith, lived there until its demolition in 1933. By the early 1900s the house may well have been too big to be run by one family and the street directories of the time also list a Mr. Jowett, partner in the firm of Jowett, Waterhouse & Co., wine and spirit merchants of 8 Clegg Street, Oldham and John Wild as living at the house, so it seems likely that the property may have been split into separate dwellings.

Abbeyhills House was demolished in April 1933 as work on extending the main road to Ashton-under-Lyne and the new housing estate got under way. This busy thoroughfare and route through to Tameside now occupies what was once the farmland of prosperous farmer and coal merchant, William Wrigley. But the house lives on through the road, which was named after it, even though most of the 'new' estate has now been pulled down.

Birch Hall, Lees

Birch Hall really does rank as one of Oldham's most interesting mansion houses. The building is shrouded in mystery and scandal and entwined with the lives of the rich and famous. A structure of amazing historical contrasts, it has been host to one of Oldham's most important personages, as well as the home of a lawbreaker.

The twists and turns in the history of Birch Hall start in the first part of the 19th Century. Edward, the son of Peter Seville of Milking Green Mill, built Birch House, sometimes called Birch Hall, around 1830 in nine acres of land at the top of Rhodes Hill, Lees. In fact, both Milking Green and the Seville names still live on. Adjacent to High Street (A669) lies Seville Terrace within sight of the Hall. In the opposite direction, near Rhodes Hill, lies the small Milking Green Industrial Estate. At the time of writing this book, the Milking Green Industrial Estate consists of a number of small units, housing a variety of micro businesses.

The fabric of the original building was red brick with stone dressings and the style of construction, in keeping with the revival of the mid-18th Century, was Gothic[6]. Two closes called the Rhodes Hey and the Middle Rhodes Hey formed the site of the house and the grounds, whilst the Further Rhodes Hey was left as meadowland.

Edward married Emily Jane Taylor, the daughter of the late William Taylor of Manor House, Springhead, on the 23rd April 1840 in Ashton-under-Lyne. The Census taken the following year contains no reference to the property, but in December 1841, Edwin Butterworth's 'History of Ashton-under-Lyne' states Rhodes Hey to be a "recently built hall in the Elizabethan style". But this is not the only mystery associated with the new Seville family as records show. Although the 1851 Census does list Birch Hall and shows Emily Jane Seville as the 'head of the household,' widowed, aged 32, along with two daughters[7], there is no reference to Edward! Documentary evidence[8] of the time alleges that Edward was 'on the run for forgery'. In fact two years later, he was charged on the 8th October 1853 with uttering two bills of Exchange purporting to be accepted by his brother, Peter. This was a serious offence, compounded by the fact that he had run from the authorities.

---

[5] http://www.industrial-archaeology.org.uk/arev26.htm

This sad state of affairs had serious consequences for the Seville family, evident in the fact that the following year, the Mansion House of Birch was advertised as an eligible investment. It is listed[9] as consisting of:

> "A splendid entrance hall, capacious dining and drawing rooms, breakfast room, butler's pantry and kitchen on the ground floor and on the upper floors five bedrooms, one with a dressing room, bathroom, water closets, servants bedroom and storeroom. The outbuildings comprise an entrance lodge, coach house, stabling for three horses and other facilities, together with surrounding land tastefully laid out in gardens and pleasure grounds and planted with choice of shrubs and trees."

Birch House, as it was then called, was at this time in the occupation of John Radcliffe Esq., a cotton manufacturer, employing 909 hands. He was 35 years old at the time of the 1851 Census. Together with him at Birch House were his wife, Louisa, who was then 26 years old and their daughter, Constance Louisa, who was ten months old. In addition, the Radcliffes employed four live-in servants to take care of them and the house. Documents of the time[10] show the terms of his occupancy as being: "Under a lease for ten years with the privilege of extending the term to fourteen years at the yearly rent of £175." [11]The property was offered as "An opportunity for investment of a moderate capital such as seldom occurs" and was "freehold of inheritance and free from chief rent". A good but expensive investment, even by modern standards.

Around this time Edward Seville and his wife, Emily Jane, were said to have emigrated to Canada. It can therefore be assumed that Edward did not receive a custodial sentence, but that in order to start a new life and leave the stigma of prosecution behind them; they were forced to relocate to the other side of the Atlantic.

John Radcliffe was obviously happy with his situation at Birch Hall, as he was still in occupation by the time of the 1861 Census. However, by 1871 the owner is recorded as Gaylord Hadwen, a cotton spinner, employing 350 hands.[12] From existing records, we do know a few things about him and his family. The Census records him as being 41 years old and his wife, Ann, as 36. They had three daughters – the grandly named Ethelinda, aged 7; Bertha, 5; and Agnes, 3. In addition, there was a one year old; sharing the same name as his father and as with the former occupiers, the Radcliffe family, the Hadwens employed four servants. Additional research reveals that coincidently, Gaylord's family also later immigrated to Canada, via France – a strange but satisfying link with the former occupants.

In 1880 records show[13] that Birch Hall now belonged to Robert Whittaker, another master cotton spinner who owned a mill and warehouse at Manchester Road, Oldham. The evidence is that he was the actual owner of Birch Hall rather than the tenant.[14] He employed over 300 hands and was also a magistrate. One of his sons, John D. Whittaker, [15]was the next occupier but the building was again reported for sale in 1899.

Although in later years Birch Hall went into decline, for one short space of time it played a small part in the history of our nation and therefore has a special place in Oldham's history. For three significant weeks in 1899, prospective parliamentary candidate, Winston Churchill,[16] stayed there, using it as a base during his election campaign. Winston went on to become one of Britain's greatest Prime Ministers, leading the country through the Second World War and beyond – becoming a Knight in the process, as well as a Freeman of the Borough of Oldham.

The history of the house now swings from glory to mystery as the next fifty years is almost without documentation. Even Census data is unavailable. Thomas Whittaker, a cotton spinner and manufacturer, was the occupier in 1901 and on the 16th July 1903 Birch Hall was again sold by auction. It was described as being the former residence of Alderman Robert Whittaker and, afterwards, of Thomas Whittaker, his eldest son. Nothing more seems to be known about this property for half a century, a time that encompassed two World Wars and a General Strike. Whether these were factors in the loss of documentation, we can only speculate, but the fact of their absence does lend a further air of mystery to Birch Hall's domestic history.

In 1948 the house was opened as a hostel for displaced persons and two years later Arnold W. and Gertrude Shaw were said to be in possession of the place[17] and seem to have remained there for the next 6 years.

Early in 1954 Mr. and Mrs. Jack McCormick acquired the property, gave up their teaching posts and set about turning the building into a private school with lofty classrooms, science and art rooms, staff room, gymnasium, kindergarten, cloakrooms and an assembly hall. The extensive grounds were made into fine playing fields for cricket, football, hockey and netball, together with an adventure playground.

Both Mr. and Mrs. McCormick were natives of Oldham and qualified teachers. Educated at Westminster College in London, Mr. McCormick was a practical artist in almost every medium. A Fellow of the Royal Society of Art, he exhibited and sold many of his works. The McCormicks had two children and were members of Zion Methodist Church in Lees. Several thousand pounds were spent on the conversion and adaptation of the school, which opened in May 1954, with just thirty-two scholars, aged between four and fifteen years.

The junior department of the new school was based at 'Ormidale,' the McCormick's residence on nearby Lees New Road, whilst the senior department occupied Birch Hall. By 1959, with the addition of three more classrooms making eighteen in total, the school was catering for no less than 337 pupils. In November 1962 planning permission to build houses at Birch Hall was applied for, but by April 1964 a further change had occurred. 'Ormidale' was converted into a care home for the elderly and Birch Hall was taken over by Mr. and Mrs. Pennington. The private school, therefore, ceased to function. Just after this the premises were converted into a hotel with function facilities and a restaurant. It also became one of the North's top Jazz venues.

Grandiose plans for turning the building and grounds into a gigantic leisure centre with many extensions never saw the light of day and the premises, again, changed hands in 1989 when Mr. Allan Stott of Failsworth took over the ownership. The best we can establish for this time is that Mr. Stott did not live at the house. However, liquidators were called in, in August 1992 and the building survived a few more troubled years before being demolished in 2000 to make way for a new housing development. A sad ending to a remarkable dwelling.

Incidentally, 'Ormidale' changed its name to 'Lees View' in 1992 and 'Ashbourne House' four years later, but whatever its name; it still continues to be run as a care home.

6   http://en.wikipedia.org/wiki/Gothic_architecture
7   The 1851 Census also shows three live-in servants listed by name.
8   The Higson Collection at Oldham Local Studies & Archives.
9   The Higson Collection at Oldham Local Studies & Archives.
10 The Higson Collection at Oldham Local Studies & Archives.
11 http://www.measuringworth.com/calculators/ppoweruk/
     Using this calculator, a comparable figure of £11,390.66 is reached by today's prices.
12 http://pwnhc.learnnet.nt.ca/research/findingaids/N-1993-003.pdf
13 The 1880 Street Directory.
14 Textile Directory - copy at Oldham Local Studies & Archives.
15 Aged 25 at the time of the Census of 1891, which also showed him as 'head of the household,' including two other sons: Arthur, aged 18 – a medical student and Myles, aged 17 and in the Army.
16 http://www.winstonchurchill.org/i4a/pages/index.cfm?pageid=710 and
     http://www.bbc.co.uk/history/historic_figures/churchill_winston.shtml
17 See the 1948 Burgess Roll.

Blake House, 11 High Street, Lees

Blake House, 11 High Street, Lees.
©D. Gurr. Reproduced with the kind permission of D. Gurr.

Unlike many of the mill houses in this book, Blake House is still in existence, serving a purpose and forming an attractive gateway into the area. Nestling on the bank of the River Medlock, between Salem and the entrance to Lees Village, this imposing three-storey stone house, with its Georgian proportions, stands out from the surrounding red brick modern builds, lending it an air of grandeur.

There is no specific entry for Blake House in the 1841 Census; all the properties in the area are referred to as 'Lees.' Ralph Taylor, however, was resident there in 1843, which might indicate that this was the year that the house was built. He was a partner in the firm of R. & T. & G. Taylor, cotton spinners, doublers and warp makers, trading at the Springside Mill on the opposite side of the main road.

Thomas Taylor, Ralph's father, had built this mill in 1800. It appears likely that later partners were Ralph's brothers. Firstly, Thomas,[18] who was living at Blake House by the time of the 1851 and 1861 Census, with his wife, Sarah and family; they later moved further into Lees at Rhodes Hill. Secondly, brother George, of whom we know little, except that he resided at Springside House on Spring Lane. This building was later converted into a presbytery for St. Edwards Roman Catholic Church until 1960. Springside Mill burnt down on the 26th March 1884 and was replaced by Leesbrook Mill. This Mill itself is of particular interest and from the windows of Blake House you can see mounted on the wall, a blue plaque commemorating the life of Annie Kenney,[19] a prominent women's rights campaigner, at the turn of the 20th Century.

By 1870, John Ogden is listed as the occupier of Blake House. He was a retired cotton spinner living with his wife, Ann, both of whom were fifty-two years of age. Records show that they employed one live-in servant. They were still at Blake House at the time of the 1881 Census but John died on the 1st December the following year at the age of 65 years. You can still visit his burial site and see his headstone in St. John Hey churchyard.

In 1891 the building began its life as commercial premises. It was converted from a private dwelling into a doctor's residence and surgery. John Duncan McVean MB.CM.,[20] the Medical Officer for Health for Ashton-under-Lyne was living there at the time, together with his mother, Janet Alston McVean. Janet was described[21] as a 65-year-old widow, living on her own means, whilst John was aged thirty-one. The 1901 Census revealed that John Duncan McVean was now 'head of the household,' aged forty-one. It is assumed that his mother had previously died. John was now married to Hilda M., who was 22 years old and they had a month old baby called Janet A. and three servants. They were still there in 1915 and it is believed that they remained at Blake House for many more years.

There is a general lack of electoral registers for the Lees area in subsequent years, but the occupants of Blake House in 1949 were Thomas D. and Catherine McPherson Hunter, together with Gilbert H. Campbell, suggesting that at some stage the house had been divided into two separate dwellings. By 1954 William and Mary Lowergaw were living there, as well as Gilbert and Mary Flora McKinnon Campbell, again suggesting two dwellings within the one building.

We have no documentary evidence to inform us of what happened in the intervening years; however, Blake House ceased to be a residential home in 1991 when it was converted into offices. Blake House is currently occupied by a firm of solicitors - a suitably dignified use for this historical treasure.

Broomhurst

*Broomhurst, c. 1930.
© E. Perry. Reproduced with the kind permission of E. Perry.*

Between the A62 and the A627, in the area currently referred to as Coppice, you will find the site of Broomhurst. It seems terribly negligent that a house, which housed such noteworthy owners and by association played a significant part in industrial and business life at local and international levels, has not been preserved. At least one illustrious occupant changed the world we live in, as well as being a prominent employer, whose influence stretches down the years to the modern age.

This large house, which stood back from the main road near to the junction of Windsor Road and Wellington Road, was built sometime earlier than 1881, when Ann Clegg, a fifty-nine year old widow, is listed as the occupier. She lived there with two of her five children: Abraham, a cotton spinner, aged 36 and Frederick, aged 20, as well as one servant. Abraham was a partner in the firm of J. W. Clegg & Bros., cotton spinners of Mumps Mill. In addition to these two children, Ann was also mother to Charles Clegg, who lived at Greenhill, Glodwick; James W. Clegg, who resided at Mumps House near to the mill; and John E. Clegg, who lived at Blenheim House, 101 Waterloo Street. Both A. and F. Clegg are listed in the 1891 Street Directory.

It is assumed that Ann died sometime before the next Census in 1891 because Abraham was then described as 'head of the household.' Frederick was still living with his brother and, presumably as a consequence of the loss of their mother, the number of servants had risen to three. Sometime over the next ten years, using the evidence of the 1901 Census the house appears to have been split into two, the Cleggs having moved elsewhere. In one part lived Harold and Mary Wrigley with their three young children and no less than five servants. Considering that, previously, there had been no more than five people living in the entire house, ten people must have been a squeeze in only half of the house.

Sharing the property was one of Oldham's most important citizens, the founder of the large Hollinwood engineering works, Sebastian de Ferranti.[22] An electrical engineer, he had been born in Liverpool in 1864 of an Italian father and English mother. His first job was with Siemens Brothers[23] where, in 1881, he assisted Sir William Siemens in his experiments with an electric furnace making steel. At the same time he attended evening classes at University College, London.

---

[18] According to the 1851 Census (indexed under Main Street), this second Thomas Taylor, was aged 25 and a cotton spinner by trade. He had a wife named, Sarah, aged 26 and an eight-month daughter named, Elizabeth Mary. By the 1861 Census, their ages are recorded as having increased by the expected ten years and in addition to Elizabeth Mary, now aged 10, there are four other children: Edith, 9; Robert Ogden, 5; Julia Ann, 2; and Samuel at one month old. The Taylors also had two live-in servants.

[19] http://www.spartacus.schoolnet.co.uk/Wkenney.htm and http://www.oldham.gov.uk/living/planbuildmatters/plandev_home/blue-plaques.htm

[20] http://archives.li.man.ac.uk/ead/search/?operation=full&rsid=161682&firstrec=1&numreq=20&hitposition=0&highlight=1 - note this is a large archive and this entry appears about a third of the way down.

Ferranti made the first dynamo with a cordless disc in 1882, patenting it as the Ferranti alternator. It had an electrical output far greater than any of its rivals. In 1887, he became chief electrician to the newly formed London Electric Supply Corporation, resigning in 1892 to devote his time to private business and founded Ferranti Ltd. at Hollinwood. Siding with electrical pioneer Nicola Tesla against his great rival Thomas Edison, Ferranti became a pioneer of high voltage AC systems. He was also the originator of long distance transmission of high-tension electric current.

Although he only remained at Broomhurst for a few years, Ferranti's mark was to be felt in the Oldham area for many years to come, with the firm going from strength to strength and employing hundreds of workers. He died in 1930 at the age of 66 years and was buried in the same grave as his parents and his daughter, Yolanda, at Hampstead Cemetery, London. Despite the changing fortunes of Ferranti in recent times,[24] the name still lives on in Oldham and the various devolved divisions of Ferranti still employ significant numbers of Oldhamers.

The Wrigleys were still in residence at Broomhurst in 1905 but within five years another change in occupation took place when Sidney Stott,[25] the architect was living at the house. He was the fourth of five children, born in Chadderton on 20th February 1858, neither to wealth or poverty. His father was an established architect in Oldham and Sidney became, undoubtedly, Oldham's greatest architect, designing twenty-two cotton mills in the borough and fifty-five elsewhere in Lancashire. This accounted for 44% of the total spinning capacity of the county between 1887 and 1925. His mills can be identified by the use of two corbelled rings, instead of the usual one, on the chimneys. He was always known as Sidney up until 1920; but upon being made a baronet, he adopted the title of Sir Philip Sidney Stott, possibly thinking that a title made up of three 'Ss' was too much of a mouthful!

In 1906, Stott purchased the greater part of Stanton village in the Cotswolds, and helped it become one of the most distinguished villages in the area. For example, he was responsible for the installation of both water and electricity there. He left Broomhurst in 1913 and moved to Stanton Court, a large mansion house in the village, until his death in 1937, although he still attended his Oldham office until 1921. He eventually became the Lord Lieutenant of Gloucestershire.

John Stafford Nuttall and his wife, Mary, appear on the Burgesses Roll for 1918, although the following year it is their son, Gerald Lees Stafford Nuttall, who is listed. The inclusion of the name Lees[26] may denote ties with families of that name, an old and established one in the Oldham area; or possibly links with the area of the same name. Whichever, it would not be unreasonable to assume that there is some local link, given that it is an unusual middle name.

The last occupiers of this fine house appear to be Henry and Alice Ada Hood, who were resident between 1925 and 1930 and possibly a little longer, although other Burgess Rolls are not too clear.

The building was demolished around 1934, a time of significant development throughout Oldham, and replaced by a small development of houses, appropriately called 'Broomhurst Avenue.' Broomhurst House may have gone, but its influence can still be felt through the commemorative street name and the legacy of its most important occupants, Sebastian de Ferranti and Sir Philip Sidney Stott.

[21] In the 1891 Census
[22] http://www.iee.org/OnComms/Branches/UK/England/NorthE/Mersey/ferranti.cfm
[23] http://www.siemens.co.uk/index.jsp?sdc_p=ft6mls6u20o1336619i1301569pc192z2
[24] http://www.msim.org.uk/customPages/FramesContentFrame.asp?menuid=732
[25] http://www.chadderton-hs.freeuk.com/sir_philip_sidney_stott.htm and
     http://www.chadderton-hs.freeuk.com/page13-listed-bldgs.htm

Clarksfield

Lower Clarksfield House, c. 1910.

Up to this point, each house has been considered almost in isolation, with detail on the occupants and the actual building. However, in some cases, old halls in the Oldham Borough have grown up very much as a result of the use of the surrounding land and as such are inseparable from it. Higher and Lower Clarksfield, as well as Keverlow Farm are such buildings. They arose in response to the growth of wealth associated with the estate of Clarksfield and are linked to each other and the surrounding countryside.

Clarksfield[27] is the name of a large estate situated in the eastern borders of the township of Oldham, about two miles distant from the Town Centre and divided into Lower and Higher Clarksfield. It was bounded on the west side by what is now Balfour Street and lay to the north side of Side o' th' Moor, now Lees Road. The northern boundary of the estate is Greenacres Old Road (pronounced, but not exclusively, as 'Grinnikers', although this name has existed since 1633).

Lower Clarksfield, the original mansion, commanded an extensive view of the vale of the River Medlock, as well as a prospect of the Cheshire and Derbyshire hills and the mountain scenery of Greenfield and Standedge. Wellyhole and Constantine Streets constituted the eastern boundary; Wellyhole refers to an earlier siting of a well on this part of the estate and also to the house occupied in 1748 by Captain Edmund Ogden of Wellyhole. Ogden Street and the former Edmund Street were named after him. Constantine was also historical. The Reverend Robert Constantine was the incumbent of Oldham Parish Church in 1654 and continued in undisturbed possession of the living for several years. He was a faithful and laborious minister, strongly in favour of Congregationalist principles, but not sufficiently enlightened to be tolerant towards his opponents, falling out with the powers that be. In 1662 an act of Parliament required that before St. Bartholomew's Day (24th August), every minister in the church should conform to the rites and ceremonies of the Episcopal religion. Mr. Constantine declined to accede to such conditions and was deprived of his benefice. He resorted to delivering private addresses to, mostly, Nonconformist people in the Greenacres area. In 1672 he took out a license to preach from a thatched house and was largely responsible for the building of the first Greenacres Congregational Chapel at the top of what is now Constantine Street. After the death of his wife, Frances (nee Ashton), on March 29th 1695, he moved to Manchester where he spent the remainder of his life, dying in December 1699.

During the reign of King Henry VIII, the Clarksfield Estate, which covered a large part of the land to the eastern end of Oldham, belonged to George Bothe or Booth of Ashton-under-Lyne. One of his tenants was the Lees family,[28] who farmed the estate and from them, the nearby village of Lees possibly received its name.[29]

The history of Clarksfield Estate is populated with generations of people who all seem to bear the same name – and in at least one case, people of the same name who are not even related! Sir George Booth, Bart[30] of Dunham Massey, grandson of the above mentioned George, sold the estate in 1625 to his tenant, John Leeze, who having married one of the daughters of the Andrew family, had succeeded in amalgamating two of Oldham's oldest, established families. John Leeze died in 1684 and was succeeded by his grandson, John, a gentleman, who himself died in 1724. His son, another John Lees, gentleman, passed the

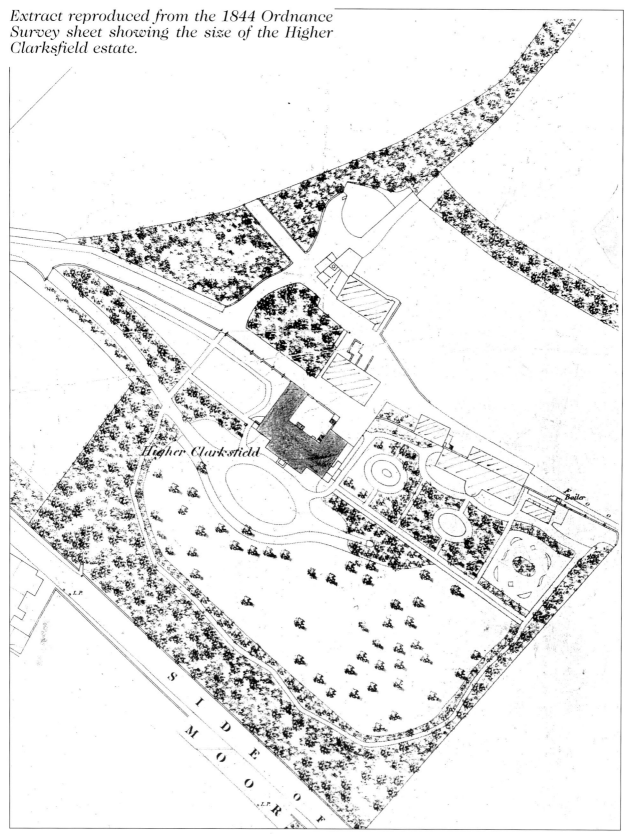

property in 1750 to his son who was yet another John. Tradition ran deep in this part of Oldham!

Upon the death of this latter John Lees (whom one might refer to as John Lees IV) in 1815, the estate descended to yet another John Lees, a banker of Fairfield, Droylsden. This hamlet, which houses a most interesting Moravian settlement can still be seen today and is at its most charming during Christmas when the Cristingle festival attracts visitors from all over the Manchester area. This John Lees was not a direct family member of the former owners.[31] An admirer of the settlement, John Lees decided to build the Moravian Church and School at Salem,[32] close to where the original family mansion house of Lower Clarksfield was situated in 1824. Since the Moravian Church is still in existence (and still serves a lively and active community), we can deduce that Lower Clarksfield House was beyond the junction of Glen Road and Clarksfield Street, off the A669.

The heirs to the estate were Joseph and James Lees who were master cotton spinners and manufacturers at Clarksfield Mill, lying further down the hill. James was also the principal partner in the coal-mining operations of Messrs. Lees, Jones, Booth and Co. and was resident at Lower Clarksfield. In 1827 his son built a more modern mansion, Higher Clarksfield, in the midst of fertile and well-planted grounds nearer to Oldham and, around this time, he also laid the first stone of St. James's Church on Greenacres Moor.[33]

The Ordnance Survey Map of 1848 shows the Clarksfield estate of the Lees family occupying a considerable length of Side o' th' Moor, our present Lees Road. It started at Cow Lane near to Balfour Street; where there was a lodge to admit visitors to a long drive leading up to Higher Clarksfield House. The house was fronted by lawns, with trees hiding it from the gaze of travellers passing along Side o' th' Moor. A footpath connected Higher and Lower Clarksfield, crossing the line of the present Clarksfield Road, then little more than a path across the field leading to Greenacres Cemetery.

Keverlow Farm, referred to above (or Caverlow as it was sometimes spelt), disappeared when the railway line to Delph was established in 1856, but the name is preserved in Keverlow Street. With the quick build-up of industry taking place, factories, mills and houses spread along Side o' th' Moor from Mumps and eventually covered most of the grounds of Higher Clarksfield. A later descendent of the Lees family of Clarksfield, Alice 'Ailsie' Mary Lees, married Arthur Edward Wrigley in 1901 and went to live at 'Woodfield' (see separate entry). This dynastic alliance is evident from the fact that Arthur was a partner of the Lees and Wrigley cotton empire at Greenbank Mill, Glodwick.

Higher Clarksfield eventually became so surrounded by houses that it became two separate dwellings - Nos. 61 and 63 Keverlow Street, which can still be seen. The original building has an interesting cornice and parapet, with new windows inserted in older openings and an additional entrance made in a former window opening. These modern changes have been done with some sensitivity and because of this; they still remain pleasing residences, interestingly sited in the middle of the later built terraced housing. A shadow of their earlier illustrious history, it would be interesting to know if the current occupants and adjoining residences know just how illustrious these properties were in their heyday.

In the 1930s the Ramsden family occupied Lower Clarksfield but the premises became unoccupied just before the Second World War. Doing its part in allowing Oldhamers to 'Dig for Victory', the gardens were covered by allotments and hen-pens. Lower Clarksfield House was demolished in the 1980s and replaced by a modern residence near to the junction of Clarksfield Street and Glenfield Close.

This timeline of the Clarksfield Estate gives us an interesting insight into both the speed of growth attributable to the Industrial Revolution in this area, but also to the effect this would have had socially and on the landscape. To the extent that the housing eventually crowds out the originators of the wealth, making them victims of their own success. Clarksfield is now predominantly a sea of Victorian houses, retaining just the smallest vestiges of its Georgian origins, in the shape of Higher Clarksfield and the Moravian Church. Modern day Clarksfield is a true monument to the success of the mill owners and the durability of their legacy.

The name of Clarksfield nowadays applies not only to this extensive estate but also the district on the other side of Lees Road, stretching back as far as Roundthorn and Glodwick Lows. The latter name is very ancient with the first reference to Glodic (as it is still pronounced today) as long ago as 1190, although over the years it has been spelt in many different ways. The present spelling of the name (with the 'w' silent) was recorded for the

Extract reproduced from the 1891 Ordnance Survey sheet showing the relative positions of Higher and Lower Clarksfield Houses.

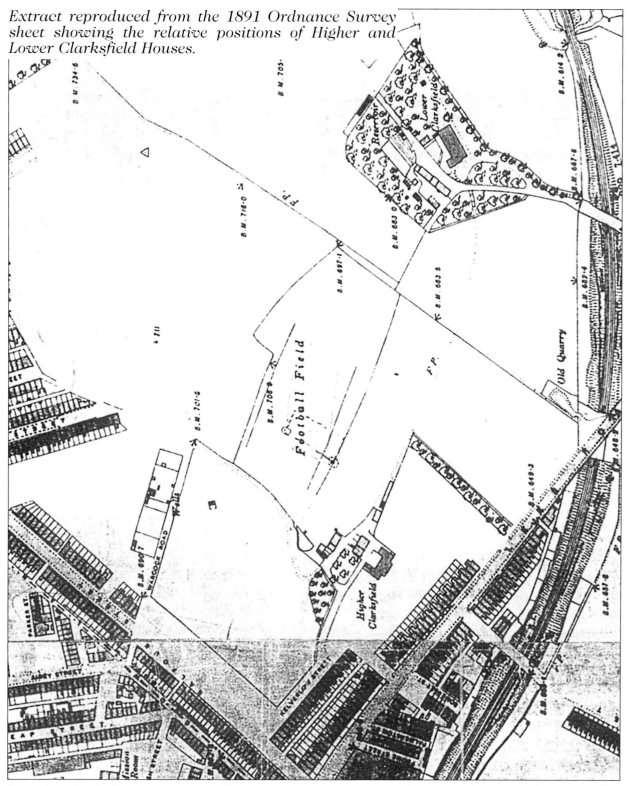

first time in 1633 and is probably a corruption. Its origin lies in a Celtic settlement called Glod after the dike, which drained the old Roman Road. The Anglians added their own word 'dic' which also referred to a dyke.

26 http://genforum.genealogy.com/lees/
27 The following three paragraphs are extracted from: 'History if the Ancient Parochial Chapelry of Oldham,' by the Rev. George Perry-Gore; 'Historical Sketches of Oldham,' by Edwin Butterworth (1856) and 'a History of Oldham,' by Hartley Bateson (1949).
28 http://www.manchester2002-uk.com/history/old-families4a.html
29 This is only hearsay, but seems to be highly likely.
30 See reference in the introduction to this book.
31 As far as can be ascertained.
32 Salem is believed to be a contraction of the word Jerusalem, most aptly given the cultural mix of the area, a centre of faith for Christians and Muslims, as well as Jews.
33 http://www.genuki.org.uk/big/eng/LAN/Oldham/StJames.shtml

Copster House

Copster House c. 1902.

Originally called Copster Hill, according to Edwin Butterworth,[34] this estate contained a commodious old habitation belonging to the Bent family. The area around the junction of the main A6104 to Ashton-Under-Lyne and the B6192 leading towards Werneth is still identified today as Copster Hill.

Copster Hill was built in 1711 as recorded on a date stone,[35] reading T. E.,[36] 1711. Having said that, it is possible that the house was built onto a much older cottage, of which we have very little information, forming part of the rear of the property.

Thomas Bent, of Copster Hill, was a chapman; another name for a peddler or hawker. Despite the apparent lowliness of this occupation, it would appear that he owned the property and upon Thomas' death on March 22nd 1739,[37] the house passed down to John Bent. We do not know the precise relationship between Thomas and John, but they were possibly father and son.[38] However, we do know that John was in possession of the house in 1759.[39] Subsequently, either he or one member of the family sold the property to the Kershaws, farmers of Top-of-Green, Hollins, who were related to the Kershaws who had lived at Whetstone Hill, since at least 1621 – part of the area we now refer to as Derker. The dates for this period are uncertain and all we really have is a sequence of events that cannot be pinned down firmly in time.

Somewhere in the intervening 50 years, the house came into the possession of John Kershaw of Copster Hill. Identified as a yeoman, in this case the title implies a landowner. John died February 21st 1793.[40] He was the father of Ralph Kershaw, gentleman, who died unmarried on November 5th 1809 and who is stated to have devised legacies of £15,000 each to his two nieces.[41] This was a handsome sum, equating in terms of buying power to three quarters of a million pounds in the present day.

At this point, the already complicated history becomes even more so, as family names change through marriage. Ralph had a sister, Betty, to whom the estate passed. However, as was the convention of the time, the estate was then conveyed, upon marriage, to her husband, Jonah Harrop, gentleman, of Bardsley. When Jonah died on May 22nd 1814, he left several heirs: Jonah Harrop Jnr. J.P. of Bardsley; Mrs. Joe Sidebottom of Harewood Lodge, Mottram and Mrs. William Sidebottom of Waterside, Mottram. It is assumed that the estate was settled and the house sold as part of it.

Sometime around the late 1860s, the firm of Schofield and Broome, cotton doublers and warp makers, commenced their business at Hathershaw Mill, Copster Hill, a premises that still houses industry today. George R. Broome, one of the partners, who had previously resided at 83 King Street, Oldham, moved into Copster Hill sometime between 1870 and 1875[42] and it is very likely he, who re-named the building Copster House, as references to this name seem to start at around this time. He is listed as being resident there in the 1875 Street Directory of the town. By 1880, George Kelsall Broome, his son, was living at Copster House and had been made a partner of the firm, thus indicating the probability that the elder George had either retired or died.

Four years later, and indicating a continued upward trend in the success of the business, a twining shed extension was erected at Hathershaw Mill. George Kelsall Broome, now aged 48 years, was still living at Copster House and now his wife, Jane, who was four years younger, and their four children, are also recorded. The Broome family employed two live-in servants.[43] In 1891 they were still there, although only two of their children were, by then, still at home.

The firm continued to flourish and houses built adjacent to the mill became known as Schofield Street. George Broome Jnr. was still residing at Copster House in 1895, but by 1901 the occupier was listed[44] as John Mayall. However, sometime during the next two years Jackson Brierley, an Oldham Alderman and the principal partner of the estate agents at 85 Union Street, Oldham, became the new owner of the property. Businesses bearing his name still thrive in Uppermill and Rochdale, though not at 85 Union Street, which now houses a firm of accountants. How long he stayed at Copster House is not absolutely certain but between 1910 and 1924 George James Lansdell[45] was in occupation of the house.[46]

The original house was pulled down sometime around the 1930s, during that major time of redevelopment that saw the sweeping away of a number of Georgian and Victorian mill houses. It was replaced by a more modern building, approached by a driveway on the A6104 – Hollins Road. This house later became the home and surgery of Alexander W. Hendry and S. Brown Hendry, physicians and surgeons. They were certainly still there in 1956, but a Dr. Mulholland later took over the practice. The house itself survived until the year 2000 when it was sold and demolished as part of a proposed new housing development.

The cotton business at Hathershaw Mill continued to trade under the name of Schofield and Broome until ceasing production in 1935. During the Second World War the factory was used by the Admiralty and afterwards, for a number of years, the manufacture of handbags took place there. The building is currently used for precision plastic moulding. Despite the demise of Copster House as a residence, it is remarkable and uplifting that one of the mills associated with it still continues to survive and provide jobs in the area, despite the changes of a century and a half.

Croft Bank House, Rochdale Road, High Crompton

Croft Bank House, High Crompton, c. 1910. © J. Maiden. Reproduced with the kind permission of J. Maiden.

Each of our houses is unique, not only in its conception and history, but also in its ultimate fate. Of them all, Croft Bank House seems to be the saddest in that its history was bound up for so long with the fortunes of its founding family. With the ending of the dynasty, came the end of the house and with it a part of Oldham's heritage.

[34] http://www.lancs.ac.uk/depts/history/research/baines.htm
[35] The house and the date stone are now gone.
[36] Where the T. E. might be all that was left of T. E. B. – initials of Thomas E. Bent.
[37] Source: 'Historical Sketches of Oldham' by Edwin Butterworth, 1856.
[38] Source: 'Historical Sketches of Oldham' by Edwin Butterworth, 1856.
[39] Source: 'Historical Sketches of Oldham' by Edwin Butterworth, 1856.
[40] Source: 'Historical Sketches of Oldham' by Edwin Butterworth, 1856.
[41] Source: 'Historical Sketches of Oldham' by Edwin Butterworth, 1856.
[42] Copster Hill was unoccupied in 1871, at the time of the Census.
[43] Source: the Burgess Roll.
[44] Source: the 1901 Census.
[45] http://www.historyscape.org.uk/
[46] Source: the Burgess Roll

This large house, once situated on the left hand side of Rochdale Road approaching High Crompton (B6194), was built by Joseph Clegg, part of the large Clegg family[47] who owned land and property in the district, including High Crompton cotton spinning mills. What little we know about the architecture of the house can be gleaned, in part, from existing photographs and what can be imagined from the status of the occupants and the style of the time - that it was a substantial property, built of stone, with surrounding grounds.

Joseph Clegg was born in 1817,[48] the eldest son of John and Hannah Clegg (nee' Travis). It is thought that 'Croft Bank House' was built sometime in the early 1870s. Joseph and his wife, Harriett, the daughter of Joseph Wild[49] were married around 1842 and had a total of six children. At the time of the 1861 Census, their ages were recorded as: John, 18 years old; Henry, 15; Joseph, 14; Mary T., 11; James W., 7; and Hannah who was 9.

Documentation[50] leads us to believe that the Clegg family lived in the house for a number of years, albeit in a fluid form. The 1875 Street Directory for Crompton lists both Joseph and his brother, Edwin. The Street Directory for 1880, five years later, refers to Joseph as well as two of his sons, Henry and James.

A year later, the 1881 Census records Joseph Clegg as 63 years old, with his wife, Harriett, a year older. James Wild Clegg (note the inclusion of Harriett's family name for their youngest son – a delightful tradition and a boon to historians), is the only one of their children to still be living at home, unmarried, aged 27 and a cotton spinner. However, with just the three adults living at Croft Bank House, the record shows that they still retained three servants who 'lived in' at the house.

After Joseph's death in 1885, his son Henry moved back to Croft Bank House, presumably to act as head of the house and take care of his aging mother. The 1891 Census states that Harriett is a 74 year old widow, living on her own means and Henry is a single forty-four year old cotton spinner. Interestingly, Henry's sister, Mary T., has also moved back to the family home, aged 41 years and the Census states that she was living on her own means. We do not have any specific details on why this might be – but it is not inconceivable that she was widowed and returning home for the support and comfort of her family and familiar surroundings.

It is known that both Harriett and Henry remained at Croft Bank until at least 1894, but the 1901 Census lists the eldest son, John, as the occupier, by which we can imagine that mother, Harriett, had died. Whilst this may have been the case for Harriett, we have no record of the fates of either Henry or sister Mary. John was described as a widower, aged 58 years, his wife, Sarah Ann (nee' Fitton), having died. The Burgess Roll for 1905-6 still lists John as the occupier, but he died in the latter year, at the age of sixty-three. John's son, Arthur, took over the occupancy of the house, following his father's death. We know very little about Arthur in terms of his occupation or marital status, although he was likely to have been a cotton spinner. We do know that he remained at the house until his own death in 1919.

After 1919, there is very little documentation in relation to the house, which means we can only speculate about its last years. It is thought that the house was possibly vacant until its demolition sometime in the 1930s – as we know this was a time of great change for Oldham and one at which a large number of mill owners houses were levelled in the name of progress. If you take a walk along Rochdale Road, you can see for yourself the original gateposts of Croft Bank House still bearing the name. To one side, the former lodge building at the end of the drive is still in existence; but the main site, for so long the home of the Clegg family, is now occupied by modern bungalows.

[47] http://www.clegg-family.net/research2.html (16th March 2007)
[48] The Clegg genealogy is well researched and a copy is available to view at the Oldham Local Studies and Archives.
[49] http://www.geocities.com/Heartland/Plains/6821/1871Wild.htm
[50] As before a visit to Oldham Local Studies and Archives will reveal the well-researched Clegg family tree.

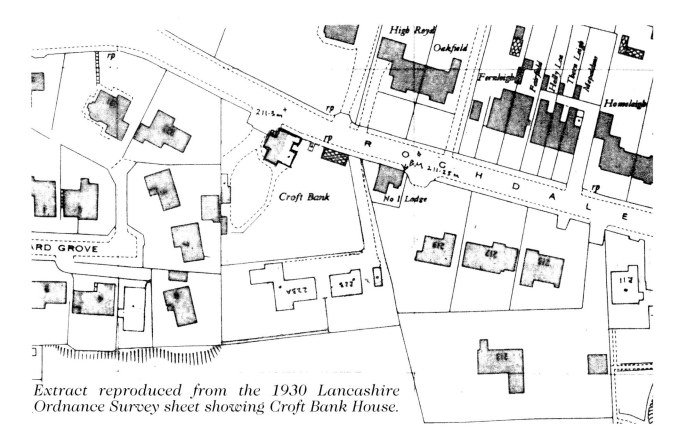

Extract reproduced from the 1930 Lancashire Ordnance Survey sheet showing Croft Bank House.

Crompton House

Crompton House, 2007.
©D. Gurr. Reproduced with the kind permission of D. Gurr.

Whilst many of the featured estates on which fortunes were based have histories dating back to the time of the Tudors and before, none of the individual houses in this book have the pedigree of Crompton House. This imposing house standing on the right hand side of Rochdale Road, High Crompton, was formerly, as the name suggests, the home of the Crompton family. The family themselves had been mentioned in historical documents since the 13th Century[51] – to put this into context and demonstrate its antiquity, some of the major world events of that time include the signing of The Magna Carta by King John (1215), the preaching of St. Frances of Assisi (d.1226) and the recapture of Jerusalem by Islamic Knights. For all the uncertainty that can creep into a history of this length, we are certain that a Crompton Hall existed in the Shore Edge area in 1442.[52]

The long timescale associated with this family, yields a wide range of historical data. But in relation to the current building, its true history can be said to have started more recently - in the late 17th or early 18th Century. Samuel Crompton of Whitfield who died in 1658[53] was the ancestor of the donors of the original school building. Whilst none of the 13th Century property pertaining to the Crompton family survives as part of this estate, there is a building, which contains a 1710 date stone, a possible clue as to its date of erection. At this point, we must again leap forward in time in order to establish the most recent history of this outstanding Oldham building and learn how it is tied up with other major landmarks in the Borough.

23

The last male member of the Crompton family was Captain Abram Crompton, brother of Alice Milne and one of the partners of A & A Crompton and Co., owners of Park and Woodend cotton mills at Wrens Nest.

On the occasion of the Coronation of King George V on June 22nd 1911, Captain Abram Crompton presented to Crompton Urban District Council the land on which Dunwood Park was built. This legacy was on behalf of himself and his nephews, namely, James Crompton Cheetham, Joshua Milne Crompton Cheetham and John Crompton Cheetham. The park itself was opened on September 14th 1912 – note the inclusion of the name Milne linking to the family into whom his sister had married. We are not told what, if anything, Alice inherited, but the future of the family runs through Alice's line.

Twelve years later, in 1924, the government of that time decided that separate schools should be established for all senior scholars from the age of eleven years. Almost immediately Miss Catherine Cocker of New Bank, Heyside, whose mother had been Catherine Crompton,[54] voiced her concern regarding the education of senior scholars from church schools. Unfortunately she died[55] before she could take any action in the matter, leaving her sister, Mrs. Anne Ormerod, and her cousin, Miss Mary Crompton as inheritors of the Crompton estates.[56]

In June of that year Mary and Anne wrote to the Rural Dean of Oldham stating that they would be willing to give Crompton House to the Association of Church Voluntary Schools in Oldham, for the purpose of providing a Higher Standard Centre School for scholars over the age of eleven. This was matched with a Trust Fund providing £1,000 a year, a magnificent sum of money in those days and equal in buying power of almost £40,000 by today's standards. The Crompton Local Authority, backed by the Lancashire Education Committee at Preston, at first resisted this idea, preferring to pursue plans to build their own senior school in the town. They even went as far as suggesting that there would never be enough children in the area to fill two senior schools. The proposal for the new school at Crompton House survived all these arguments; however, and in August 1925 the building and grounds, together with an endowment of £20,000 (worth something like £784,000 today) for maintenance, were handed over to the custody of the Manchester Diocesan Board of Finance. The County Education Authority meanwhile went ahead with the building of their own 'Central School' in Kings Road - which later became New Barn School.

Crompton House School was officially opened on the 29th September 1926 by the Dean of Manchester – Dr. Hewlett Johnson, and two days later the school admitted its first twenty-five pupils on a voluntary basis. Within a very short time, it became necessary to enlarge the school to meet the request of the Board of Education that Crompton House and Crompton Central Schools should find places for all local children over eleven years of age. These extensions enabled the school to cater for 330 pupils and set the pattern persisting to the present day of always trying to extend, alter and improve the facilities at the school to meet need.

Today, Crompton House remains a popular choice amongst parents throughout the Metropolitan Borough of Oldham and areas beyond and is almost always over subscribed. Its high academic achievement and reputation for nurturing and supporting its pupils make it an outstanding school and a worthy successor to both the historic name and location.

51 http://www.scholiast.org/history/timetables/1200s.html (Available online and accessed March 2007)
52 http://en.wikipedia.org/wiki/Crompton_Hall (Available online and accessed March 2007)
53 Researched by Frances Stott, historian and former librarian for Oldham Libraries.
54 Consult the Crompton family tree for clarification on the complicated inter-family relationships.
55 Miss Catherine Cocker died in 1924.
56 A copy of this rather complicated family tree can be viewed at Oldham Local Studies and Archives.

Crossbank House, Lees

No doubt some younger readers, and indeed perhaps some of the older ones, might be tempted to ask, 'Where is Crossbank?' and so a little explanation might be useful at the start.

Crossbank was, until the amalgamation with Lees Urban District Council in 1894, a small hamlet lying in the extreme northern tip of the Parish of Ashton-under-Lyne, joining Saddleworth at Austerlands and Waterhead, near to the Temple and Bowling Green Inn, with its southern boundary joining up with Hey Village. The present day location might be as near the junction of the A62 Huddersfield Road and Stamford Road leading from Lees Village.

In common with a number of estates associated with the halls in this book, there is much evidence to show that Crossbank existed long before the village of Hey. It is mentioned in the Rate Assessment of King James I in 1618, along with all the other villages that comprised, at the time, the Parish of Ashton-under-Lyne, whereas there is no mention of Hey.[57] Right up until the end of the 19th Century, the area of Crossbank was very much out in the country. A farm stood at the Waterhead end of what is now Stamford Road, with a few larger type houses further down towards Hey. Another settlement, up on the hillside, included another farm, which ultimately became Crossbank House, the main subject of this chapter. A few stone cottages had begun to be built on the opposite side of the road, off Dunham Street, and there were three old cotton mills: Longrange, Lower and Bangor, down in the valley which locals still call to this day, 'Millbottom.' The Crossbank area name can still be found in the cul-de-sac running to the west, off Stamford Road, called Higher Crossbank.

The street names Dunham and Stamford, historically refer to major landowners from mediaeval times – the Earls of Stamford of Dunham Massey in Cheshire. Stamford Road, straight and wide, was built in 1864 to provide work for unemployed cotton mill operatives during the famine.

Crossbank Farm or House is a two-storey stone building dating from around 1743 and possibly earlier. The massive lintel over the entrance is inscribed AO EO 1743, which indicates the owners at the time as Amos and Elizabeth Ogden.[58] Its history remains, in parts, relatively undocumented, with large, tantalising gaps that can only hint at the people that have lived, and events that have taken place, within its elegant 250-year-old walls.

Today the house shows extensive signs of modernisation, but through this shine Georgian architectural gems that reveal its origins. The entrance doorway has dressed jambs, although the door itself is modern. Some lights of the chamfered mullion windows have been filled in, but others remain visible and the roof is flagged in York stone, as it would have been when constructed. A true reflection of the architectural and historical importance of Crossbank House lies in the fact that it is listed as a Grade II building. However, the fact that it has been modernised over the years to meet the changing needs of its occupants, may hold a clue to its continued existence when so many of the other houses in this book failed to make it into the second half of the 20th Century.

The 1841 and 1851 Censuses list six separate dwellings under the name of Crossbank. It might initially seem mysterious (and from an historian's perspective, perplexing) that neither of them indicate which, if any, relate to Crossbank House itself – however this is understandable when you consider that the whole area was referred to as 'Crossbank'. The 1861 Census gives us the first indication of the status and location of Crossbank House, when it states that Edward Seville, a twenty-nine year old master cotton spinner, his wife, Elizabeth, age 28, both of whom were born at Ashton-Under-Lyne were living there, with their nine month old son, Isaac, together with one employed servant. This Edward is not to be confused with a gentleman of the same name who lived at Birch Hall[59] from 1830 – c.1850 and who, by this time, was probably settled in Canada.

This Seville family were still in residence at Crossbank House in 1871 with Elizabeth having given birth to another baby, Hester May, in the interim period. The Sevilles were cotton doublers[60] and ran the firm of Isaac Seville and Sons at Coppice Mill, Waterhead, from around 1875 up until the turn of the century. The Street Directories between 1875 and 1884 list Crossbank as being in Austerlands and the occupier as Edward Seville, although a slight contradiction to this is the fact that the 1881 Census only lists Isaac Seville, Edward's son, at the time aged twenty years of age and unmarried, together with a live-in servant. Edward Seville died prior to the next Census in 1891, which lists Elizabeth as widowed, 'head of the household,' aged 57 years and living on her own means. Isaac was still living with her, aged thirty. As a reminder that our historical records are incomplete and that those extant are in themselves incomplete, here is the evidence: the Census of 1891 also discloses another son, George Edward, who had not been mentioned hitherto and was also resident. George Edward is described as being an apprentice chemist aged 18 years – so for 18 years he had managed to avoid being recorded in official documents – or equally as likely, the evidence for his existence has either not been preserved or not yet explored by Oldham's dedicated researchers.

Isaac Seville continues to be referred to in the Burgess Rolls between 1894 and 1915 and the 1901 Census lists him as retired at the age of forty and living with his wife, Kate, five years younger than her husband. By the standards of both our current age and that of the early 20th Century, forty is a young age to retire and one is left to speculate on the reasons for his retirement.

We now enter a 'dark age' in terms of evidence for the house. We know that William Buckley, a magistrate, gave his address as Crossbank, Waterhead, in 1919, but it is not clear as to whether he was actually living at the house in question, or merely using it as an official address. An Arthur Tattersall is referred to in 1924 but there is a singular lack of further street directories for a number of years. Percy Williams is thought to have been resident of Crossbank House between 1945 and 1947, and certainly Emily Williams is described as occupier in the 1950 Burgess Roll, when both Crossbank Farm and Crossbank Cottage are listed.

The current owners of the house are Raymond and Mary Buckley.

---

[57] For the etymology of the word Hey, please see Appendix: Crossbank House, Lees.
[58] This information is derived from anecdotal evidence in a book of memoirs by Frank Kershaw, 'Crossbank Recollections,' Heath Press, Manchester, 1985.
[59] See section on Birch Hall.
[60] As opposed to the more common 'single thread' cotton spinning, doubling uses the threads wound together and twisted. This system was quite common in a number of Oldham mills.

Derker Hall

The area known as Derker today, lies between the A62, B6194 and the A672 – lying to the east of Higginshaw and west to Ripponden Road at Watersheddings. Derker has been known by other spellings in the past. It was spelt Durtkar in 1604, Dertar in 1654 and, more recently, Dirtcar.[61] The area was once marshland and the name is likely to be derived from old Norse Dritr (marshy) and Kjarr (marsh covered with bushwood). The story of Derker Hall, however, is tied up not only with its geography, but also with the industrial buildings and, strangely enough, a house with an identical name!

In the 17th Century Dirtcar Estate was in the possession of the Hilton family and later the Taylor family. A date stone found on the site of the former Derker Mills was inscribed JB 1751 and possibly refers to the John Buckley who Edwin Butterworth[62] described as possessor of Derker in 1758. James Butterworth called it "an ancient and respectable looking mansion" in 1817. However, a hall erected in 1751 would not have been called 'ancient' at that time, so it begins to look as if the date stone might relate to an extension or possibly a re-build of an earlier house – or an entirely different building, a possibility suggested by the fact that there were two Derker houses at the same time.

Hilton Greaves.
©The Oldham Evening Chronicle. Reproduced with the kind permission of the Oldham Evening Chronicle.

James and Robert Greaves, sons of John Greaves, yeoman of Thorp in Saddleworth, each independently started cotton spinning and weaving concerns at Derker Mill around 1810 and it is thought that, at that time, James was living at Derker House. By 1825, the mill was jointly owned by the two brothers, together with a John Hall and Lawrence Haig. The 1841 Census refers to Dirtcar House and lists James Greaves as the 'head of the household.' He is described as a 50-year-old cotton manufacturer, living with his wife, Mary, 48 years and their five children – John, aged 23; Mary, 18; Hilton, 17; Sarah, 15; and James, 14. There was also a family servant named Mary Mills living with them at the house. A little mystery creeps into the story of Derker Hall, when we discover that records show that by 1846 the whole of Derker Mills was owned by James Greaves alone. What had become of the other three partners is not known, although we do know that James was the proud owner of a thriving business employing 300 cotton spinning hands and another 200 hundred weavers – quite an enterprise!

The 1841 Census is notorious for rounding ages up and down and so we find that in 1851, James is referred to as a 62-year-old cotton spinner and Mary is not mentioned at all. Of the children, only John, aged 34 and Daniel, aged 22 the latter being recorded for the first time. It is unknown whether this is an error in naming the child in this Census or omissions from earlier ones – such were the vagaries of the system at that time.

James, wife Mary, and John are, again, listed in 1861 but now there is direct reference to two Derker houses. The 1861 Census lists a second house as Pitbank, near the junction of Derker Street and London Road. It was occupied by Hilton Greaves,[63] son of James, aged 38 years, his wife, Margaret, who was six years younger and their three children: James, aged five; Mary H., aged 4; and Eleanor, seven months old. They also had three servants living at the house.

Hilton Greaves was a colourful character. Known popularly as 'Old Darby' because of his habit of wearing a stiff felt hat, with rounded crown and narrow brim, which had originated in the United States;[64] he built a large weaving shed extension on the mill in 1868. Street directories at that time described the residence as 'Higher Derker' and it is this building on Stoneleigh Street, which is shown in our illustration.

Hilton Greaves was a magnificent subscriber to various local charities and he used to ride with the Oldham Harriers.[65] He was responsible for building many more extensions to

Derker Mills, in 1870, 1873, 1875, 1882, 1892 and 1894.[66] As well as spinning and weaving cotton, the firm also manufactured velvet on looms.

The 1871 Census was the first record to mention Derker House (not Hall) being on Stoneleigh Street and lists Hilton and Margaret Greaves, with their enlarged family of seven children. There was no mention of Mary H., who would have been 14 years old at the time and was possibly in service somewhere, but John Hall Greaves, aged 7; Henry, 5; Arthur Hilton, 4; Cecilia Margaret, 1; and Robert Thurston, ten months, had all been born following the last Census. This increase in the number of children would account for the five servants that were now employed and living in the house.

In 1873, Hilton Greaves donated the bell for the tower at St. Stephen's Church at Lowermoor. He also built a day school on Shrewsbury Street, allowing it to be used as a Sunday School by Holy Trinity Church, Waterhead, who were seeking to expand their parish at that time. From this humble beginning eventually arose St. Ambrose Church, Derker, appropriately built on land owned by the Greaves family.

The first mention of Hilton Greaves' residence being called 'Derker Hall' appeared in the 1881 Census and, by this time, all the children appeared to have 'flown the nest,' with the exception of Robert, who was a ten year old scholar. By the 1891 Census, ten years later, there is no mention of Hilton's wife; Margaret had died in the interim period, Hilton being described as a widower. Son, James, an unmarried thirty-five year old, described as a cotton spinner and daughter, Eleanor, five years his junior, had now returned to the family home – from which we can assume that neither was married as there are not additional family members mentioned.

In his later years, Hilton Greaves retired to Hankelow in Cheshire, where he died on February 11th 1895, aged a respectable 73 years. His will makes for interesting reading. It was originally written on the 10th January 1888, but later codicils were added as close to his death as the 2nd May 1894 and the 24th January 1895. The estate duty paid was £491,425.11s.6d, an enormous sum of money in those days and equivalent to almost four million pounds in modern buying power. The executors were Henry Greaves, his son and Adam Hall Wood, a warehouseman from Reddish Mount near Stockport – again intriguing that the name Hall is mentioned as it is also the middle name of one of Hilton's brothers; might Adam Hall Wood have been related in some manner? The testator bequeathed £2,000 to his son, James, plus the Swanbach or Grange Farm Estate[67] and £5,000 each to his four daughters, Eleanor, Mary, Cecilia and Edith, plus £15,000 in trust to each of them. To his sons, Henry and Arthur, he left shares in the Lucille Gold Mining Co.[68] on account of shares in the residuary estate valued at £10,000 and the residue of his estate to his five sons, James, John, Henry, Arthur and Robert. The full account of Hilton Greaves' will can be found in the Miscellaneous Newspaper Cuttings (Volume 3, page 210) situated at Oldham Local Studies and Archives. It first appeared in the Oldham Standard on the 22nd July 1895.

The 1901 Census gives the new owner of Derker Hall as Henry Wrigley, a 64-year-old house builder. He was living there with his wife, Emma, who was 71 and their two children, Martha A., aged forty-one and Thomas N. H., a brick setter, who was 27. Derker Hall was demolished the following year. The site of the old hall remained vacant for many years before being covered by the houses built on Oban Avenue, just off Stoneleigh Street, in 1938.

The firm of James Greaves Ltd. continued to flourish for many years, although by 1947 the number of spindles had been reduced to 60,000 with 1,100 looms in operation at that time.[69] A few years later the business was incorporated as a branch of Joshua Hoyle and Sons Ltd. (Rochdale). The factory ceased all production in 1966 and the mill was demolished five years later – the end of an era. But this is not the end of the story with regard to employment on this site. The area formerly occupied by the mill was redeveloped into new style business premises in 1982 by another giant enterprise – Ferranti Ltd.[70] The modern premises still remain - although the buildings are now occupied by other firms.

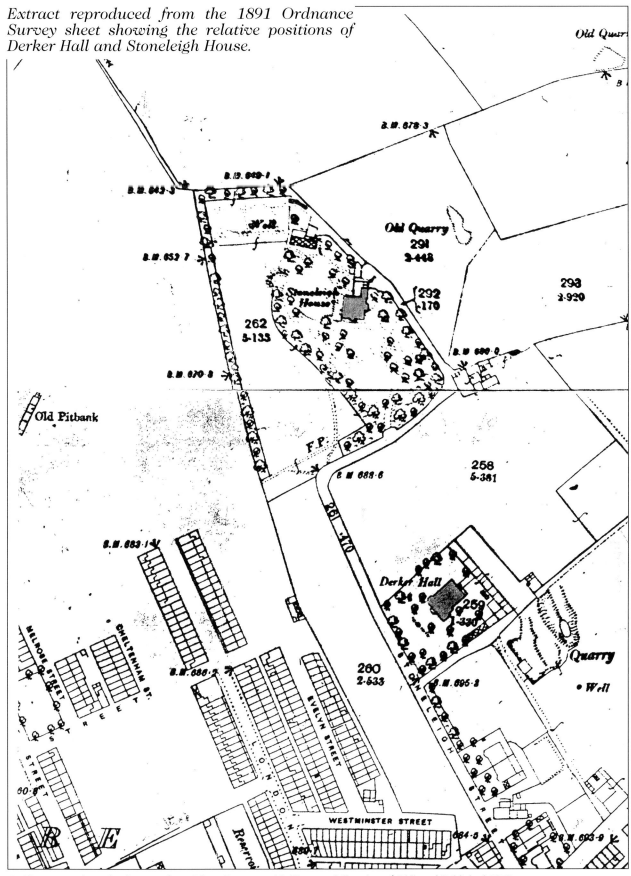

Extract reproduced from the 1891 Ordnance Survey sheet showing the relative positions of Derker Hall and Stoneleigh House.

[61] These etymological references from Edwin Butterworth's 'Historical Sketches of Oldham.' Published 1856.
[62] http://www.mcrh.mmu.ac.uk/confer/butter/abstract.htm and http://www.lancs.ac.uk/depts/history/research/baines.htm
[63] Hilton was listed as a cotton spinner and manufacturer working with his father.
[64] http://en.wikipedia.org/wiki/Bowler_hat
[65] This may be a reference to hare hunting.
[66] Source: Plans deposited at this time for approval by the local authority.
[67] Unfortunately, the whereabouts of this estate has not been established.
[68] Again, the exact location of this mine is unknown. However it is most likely to have been in South Africa.
[69] For comparison, it is known that in 1915, there were 107,000 spindles and 1,200 looms.
[70] See chapter on Broomhurst.

Downey House, Royton

Downey House, 2007.
©D. Gurr. Reproduced with the kind permission of D. Gurr.

The origins of Downey House stand out when compared to the rest of the houses in this book. Built slightly later than some of the other houses in this book, it is thought that Downey House, standing on Church Street in Royton, was erected sometime between 1825 and 1838. Still standing, it can be seen to the west of the A671 and above the B6195. Another outstanding feature lies in the fact that it was built by a lady, named Elizabeth Cooper.[71]

Elizabeth and her son, Jonathan, built the Downey Mill around this time. In the 1838 Street Directory, Elizabeth and son, Jonathan, are both described as mill owners and shopkeepers – mill owning being an unusual occupation for a woman at that time. Part of the mill was let out to other cotton concerns. At the time, it was common practice to let out whole, or part of, floors in mills to individuals for spinning, on a 'room and power' basis. This was a useful arrangement allowing people, who maybe could not afford to build their own premises, to work for themselves. They had to provide their own machinery but it was powered from the main steam engine in the mill.

By 1852 Jonathan and his brothers[72] were in sole occupation of the mill, from which it is assumed that Elizabeth had retired or more probably died. The mill employed over four hundred hands and, no doubt, one of the Cooper Brothers would have been resident at Downey House, although the property does not appear in street directories in its own right until 1871. It is, therefore, assumed that the house was deemed to be part of the fabric of Downey Mill itself. The mill was listed as being run by John Cooper and Brothers in 1861.

In 1871 the occupant of Downey House is given as James Cooper, but we have no records to suggest whether this James was a brother of Jonathan or his son. Four years later, a Miss Cooper is listed[73] and in 1880,[74] John Cooper. It is unlikely that this John was the original Jonathan, as it was already something like 55 years since Jonathan had first occupied the house. It is rendered even more unlikely by the fact that this John remained at the house until at least 1905-6. There is an addition of a Mrs. Hugh Cooper[75] also listed in 1891.

It seems as if the Cooper family might have vacated both the house and mill soon after this time, because the Beech Spinning Company Ltd. was formed in 1892 and the larger part of the mill was taken over by them and renamed Beech Mill. However, Robert Cooper was still working in part of the mill in 1908 and two years later, it was occupied by J. Wood and Co., with 12,000 spindles. The mill ceased production in the 1920s and it was described as being disued on the 1932 Ordnance Survey Map. It was later demolished, some time before the Second World War.

Despite its relative young age, Downey House did have a wonderfully Gothic feature - a mysterious feature known only to a few; there was once an underground passage connecting Downey House with the mill. What its function was and who used it we do not know and we are not even certain when its use ceased. A tantalising fact, whose mysteries may be revealed by the next generation of Oldham researchers.

Dr. W. L. Bentley,[76] who was Royton's Medical Officer of Health from 1920 until his death on the 5th October 1937, owned Downey House from around 1920. He was also in private practice for over forty years and was churchwarden at St. Paul's Church, Royton, for 25 years.

The house was sold in 1933 for conversion into an infants' school; to replace an earlier smaller building, which had been erected across the road in Chapel Croft one hundred years previously. A report of the dedication of the new school on the 22nd July 1933 stated that the building had been 'reconstructed and extended' by architect Mr. Fred Thorpe. The school opened its doors for business on the 4th September that year.

A former pupil of the school, Isabella Lowe, talking about the early part of the 20th Century, recalled in 1977: "At Downey House (then owned by the Coopers), Miss Cooper would sit by the door with a bucket full of shiny new pennies and a sack of oranges, which she would give out as we all wished her a happy New Year." It is not impossible that this is the same 'Miss Cooper' who was in residence in 1880; difficult to establish after this length of time, but a delightful thought nonetheless.

Downey House continued operating as a voluntary-aided church school until around 1969, when the new St. Paul's Junior School was erected on Hindle Drive, off Middleton Road, the B6195. The former building was amalgamated within the new school in 1998 and used as a nursery for a few years before passing to the church authorities for parish activities – a function it continues to fulfil to this day.

Entron House, Rochdale Road, High Crompton

Entron House is one of the most interesting of the houses included here, ironically, because we know the least about it. There are large gaps in the history of Entron House, but it deserves inclusion in this book on the basis that its history is linked with that of some of the most influential mill owners in the Borough during the 19th and early 20th Centuries.

The house is situated on Rochdale Road and stands back from the main road, out of sight. In fact, due to the considerable modern housing development in the vicinity, the building is now approached by a short road off Surrey Avenue, almost opposite to 'The Orchards'.

Entron House was built sometime between 1830 and 1840 by the Cocker family of New Bank House, who was one of the largest landowners in Crompton. The Cocker family was well known in the late 18th Century as local notables and benefactors of, inter-alia Holy Trinity Church, Crompton. They were also the first family in the area to use 'putting out' in the cotton industry, a practice that eventually brought an end to home spinning.

As mentioned above, their family home for many years was at New Bank House, which still stands on the east side of Oldham Road (B6194) at Heyside. An earlier ancestor was the Revd. John Thomas Cocker, gent. who lived here in 1817 about the time he acquired Swine Clough, an ancient farm a short distance to the west of Glodwick in Oldham. He subsequently offered to sell the estate for the sum of £10,750[77] to Oldham Corporation to enable the construction of Alexandra Park, on condition that the operatives temporarily unemployed in the cotton trade were used in carrying out the necessary work.

The building is a stone two-storey construction which, not surprisingly, has undergone a number of alterations; although some of the original interior features survive, justifying its rating as a Grade III listed property.

[71] The origins of this lady's wealth are unknown, but possibly inherited.
[72] The only reference to Jonathan's brothers that we have is by way of street/trade directories, which just list the firm as John Cooper and Brothers.
[73] 1875 - Street Directory, copy at Oldham Local Studies and Archives.
[74] 1880 - Street Directory, copy at Oldham Local Studies and Archive.
[75] A search through the 1891 Census of the time might well reveal what relation this Mrs. Cooper was to the brothers, but at the present this is a matter for future research.
[76] Dr. Bentley is mentioned in the Burgess Rolls and church records. There are, most likely, newspaper records of both his death and subsequent sale of the house, but we are not able to give direct references at present.
[77] Using http://www.measuringworth.com this has been calculated as having an equivalent purchasing power in today's money of £705,575.78.

Extract reproduced from the 1930 Lancashire Ordnance Survey sheet showing Entron House.

There are gaps in our early knowledge of occupancy, but the 1861 Census lists John Cocker as a 39 year old widower, a proprietor of houses and land, living at Entron House. To younger readers it may seem shocking, but is a reminder of the social and financial necessities of the time that also listed are his son, John Milne Cocker, a fifteen year old mule piecer and his daughter, Jane Mary Cocker, a twelve year old fustian cutter. Even at these tender ages, members of the family were required to earn a living and contribute to the family income, whilst learning a trade, which would stand them well in the future.

By 1870 a number of members of the Clegg family, cotton spinners of High Crompton Mills, were living at Entron House, in spite of the fact that they were not recorded in the following year's Census.[78] These included John Clegg, shortly to move to the nearby 'Croft Bank House'[79] and John Travis, Abraham, Edwin and Joshua, the first three of whom were brothers of Joseph Clegg, John's father and therefore his uncles. Ten years on, only Abraham was listed in the 1881 Census, an unmarried 51-year-old spinner and manufacturer, having one servant. By the next Census he had two servants and in 1901, no fewer than three. We have no idea what happened to the other Clegg family members and Abraham probably died at Entron House in 1907, aged seventy-eight years.[80]

It is intriguing to note that James Cocker, who was born on the 10th April 1854, was described as the owner of the property[81] for many years prior to his death in September 1921. So perhaps the Clegg family only leased the building?

James Cocker was a lover of nature, and made his estate and gardens his chief delight. He was prominently associated with Shaw Church and Sunday Schools and was one of three Conservative Councillors representing the West Ward of Crompton Council in 1919 - and probably for a much longer period. When he died he left a widow; brother, Walter; and sister, Margaret.

The unknown aspects of Entron House remain tantalising. As we stand and gaze at the outside of Entron House today, there are many questions that a 21st Century dweller might ask. What are the origins of the rather futuristic sounding name? What was the true nature of the ownership of the house? What was the relationship between the Cocker family and the Clegg family? These, and other outstanding questions posed by the gaps in the house's recorded history, remain unanswered for the next generation of historical researchers.

Fernholme, Grange Avenue

Fernholme, c. 1900.

Situated to the eastern side of Manchester Road (A62) in the modern day area known as Werneth, Fernholme was built towards the end of the 1860s, by John Taylor, a partner in the firm of J. and S. Taylor, spinners and velvet manufacturers of Primrose Bank Mill. The address at this time was Gregge Street - it was much later that it changed its name to Grange Avenue. Sadly, John Taylor Snr. must have died soon after its completion, because the 1871 Census lists his widow, Betsy, as being the 'head of the household.' There were two children living with her, John Jnr., aged 23 years and Maria, who was two years younger, together with two live-in servants. Betsy was 57 years old.[82]

John Taylor's son, John Jnr., is listed as the occupier of Fernholme in 1881. He is described as being a thirty-three year old magistrate and cotton spinner, his wife, Julia, being three years younger. Fernholme, it would appear, has always been a location associated with children – as becomes apparent in the latter half of its history. This generation of Taylors had a total of five children: John, aged 7; Charlotte, 6; Harold, 6; Julia, 3; and Frederic, just eight months. There were also no less than five servants living in with the family. By the time of the 1891 Census, evidence suggests that the property may have been divided into two separate dwellings, a not uncommon occurrence when properties became too big for a family, where children had left home, or when additional income was required. John Taylor and his family were still listed, but so also were Richard Scott Collinge, cotton spinner and manufacturer, his wife, Sarah Ann, their six children and four servants. Richard was 53 years old and Sarah was 50. Their children were called Isabella, aged 23; Edith, 21; John, 20; James, 17; Helena, 11; and Winifred, 8. Making a total of 11 children and 8 adults! Fernholme was indeed a large residence, as can be seen from the photograph.

After a stay of around forty years, the Taylor family appears to have left Fernholme sometime before 1900, because documentary evidence[83] shows that a new occupier had now joined Richard Collinge. He was Ralph Bagley, the chairman and partner in the cotton firm of Bagley and Wright, who had commenced their business with the building of

Belgrave Mill No. 1 in 1871. His success in business can be judged by the fact that he was also chairman of the Eagle Spinning Co. in Rochdale; Summervale Spinning Co. Ltd. and Stock Lane Spinning Co. respectively. He also held directorships in the Empire Spinning Co. Ltd.; Brunswick Spinning Co. Ltd. in Mossley; James Greaves Ltd.; and the North and South Insurance Co. Ltd. of Liverpool and London. A prestigious C.V. indeed!

He was also a noted religious worker and philanthropist. The 1901 Census gives his age as 61, his wife, another Betsy, was 53 and their four children were named Travis, aged 29; Clara, 22; Sissie, 17; and Alice, 12. They also had three servants living in the house.

The next decade saw a complete change in fortunes for Fernholme. The Sisters of Mercy, from nearby Werneth Grange Convent, wishing to branch out into education, purchased Fernholme in December 1911. They converted it into a high school, with the provision for thirty-two boarders. The red-brick Georgian style building, standing serene amid wandering pathways and flowered gardens, was Oldham's only convent school and taught the long-neglected values of a bygone age,[84] in spite of only being yards from bustling, modern Manchester Road.

In 1925 the boarders were transferred to Paddock House in Accrington, a distance of approximately 24 miles,[85] where the Sisters opened a grammar school. This, however, was not the end of Fernholme as an educational institution, as it then became an infant and junior school, until the outbreak of the Second World War. The premises were taken over by the local education authority as a nursery for the duration of the war, reverting back to its former use in 1946. A lake in the centre of the grounds was later drained and flagged to form a playground. This fact alone helps us to build a mental picture of the grandeur of Fernholme at its height, as the home of an important Oldham citizen.

There were still 120 pupils left at the school when it closed down on the 29th July 1983. It was later demolished and the site is now occupied by private housing called Fernholme Court and Anselm's Court.

Firs Hall, Failsworth.

Firs Hall, 2007. ©D. Gurr. Reproduced with the kind permission of D. Gurr.

The name 'Walmsley' dominated all aspects of the early existence of Failsworth right up to the 19th Century.

In 1845 Henry Walmsley, the wealthy mill owner of Gladstone Mill, purchased the land on which Pole Lane School (The Old School) was built and tried to take control of the building. He was resolutely opposed by local people

---

[78] This has been established through the Clegg family tree.
[79] See separate entry.
[80] Source: Clegg family tree.
[81] See the Burgess Roll for this period as possible source for this.
[82] Source: the 1871 Census.
[83] Source: the 1901 Census.
[84] Including, Morals, Respect for Authority and Discipline.
[85] http://www.theaa.com/travelwatch/planner_results.jsp?displaymap=true#map (Accessed March 2007)

who ultimately managed to form a committee to manage it, but had to concede that the scriptures should be used, along with other educational books, at the discretion of the teachers.

Thomas Walmsley built Firs Hall around 1850 and he also owned a corn warehouse, grocers shop and residence near to the bridge where the main Oldham Road passes over the Rochdale Canal. These buildings are still standing and in use as a restaurant.

Firs Hall, standing back from Oldham Road, near to the Brown Cow public house, is a two-storey classical building in red brick, with stone dressings and a stone porch. The forecourt drive goes round a circular garden and there are three stone gate piers at its entrance from the main road. The grounds also contain a row of large terraced houses in separate occupation. The hall was once known locally as 'Pinch Beggar's Hall,' due to the unpopularity of Henry Walmsley and his miserly characteristics and nefarious activities. Walmsley himself was called 'Harry the Swell' and he, and his family, owned a large number of buildings in the locality.

Henry Walmsley managed the Gladstone Mill and his brother, Jonathan, ran the shop and corn warehouse. Henry, or Harry as he was better known, paid his seven hundred plus workforce by cash and slips, the latter being able to be spent only in Jonathan's shop. Although it is known that both Henry and Jonathan lived at Firs Hall for a number of years, the 1861 Census lists Ann Walmsley as the 'head of the household.' She was described as a 57-year-old widow and also living in the house was Mary Taylor, aged 49 and unmarried. There were in addition, two servants. We have no idea of the relationship between the sets of women and the men in this arrangement.

Ten years later in 1871, Firs Hall was not referred to in the Census at all, and by 1881 a new family was in residence. Thomas Mellor was a 73-year-old tanner and cotton spinner. Living with him was his 62 year old wife, Alice, and their three grown up children: James, a leather factory employee, aged 30; Robert, a tanner, aged 28; and Alice A., their 23 year old unmarried daughter. Within the Census there is also reference to a 'visitor' residing with them, though no details are given. Thomas Mellor was a Justice of the Peace.

In 1891, the property seems, again, to have been vacant as there is only reference to three servants living there within the Census of that year.

By 1896 Samuel Johnson is mentioned as being the owner of Firs Hall, although five years later the Census does not mention him. Instead the 'head of the household' was described as Hannah Johnson, aged 56, most probably Samuel's wife. She was living at Firs Hall with her seven children: John, aged 22, a cotton spinner; Elizabeth and Alice, both seemingly aged 20 and therefore possibly twins; Samuel Jr., aged 19, another cotton spinner; Annie, aged 17, a pupil teacher; James A., aged 15 and Lillian G., aged 10, both scholars. Strangely, Samuel Johnson Snr. appears in the electoral registers of 1902, 1903 and 1906, leading to the conclusion that possibly Samuel had been away from home at the time of the Census of 1901. Firs Hall continues this fade in and out of history as it fails to appear in the registers for 1909 and 1910 – though it is believed that the Johnson family lived there during this period.

By 1913, the delightfully named Agnes Cuthbertson Kidney is referred to as the owner of the property, but the only other pre-war register in 1934 again makes no reference to Firs Hall. Its absence from small patches of history remains a mystery.

Firs Hall will be remembered during the Second World War as being used as a welfare centre and school clinic. The original building has been much altered and several extensions made during the 1980s and 1990s. It is currently used as a residential rest home for elderly people.

Higher House, Rochdale Road, Royton

Higher House, c. 1910

John Francis Mellor, a solicitor and magistrate, built Higher House[86] at the junction of Rochdale Road, Sandy Lane and Dogford Road, Shaw around 1855. By today's standards, his family was exceptionally large. But viewed against the birthrate at the time,[87] the fact that he and his wife had no fewer than eleven children was not considered excessive; however, the fact that they were all sons makes it far more so.

The 1872 Burgess Roll for the district lists John and Ralph Mellor as occupiers of the building, whilst three years later, in the Street Directory, it is Robert Mellor alone. In 1876, this Robert Mellor built Highfield cotton mill on Bleasdale Street and was still being listed as the occupier in 1894. By 1899-1900, however, Higher House was occupied, rather confusingly, by another John Francis Mellor who was almost certainly related.

Highfield Mill ceased production in 1903 and laid empty for twelve months before being purchased by the Park Mill Ltd. (Royton) and re-named Park No. 1 Mill; a second mill being erected alongside it in 1912 – the house remaining unaffected by this new mill building. By the latter time, Arthur S. and Hannah Jane Mellor were already resident in Higher House and the building appears to have remained in the Mellor family ownership for a number of years.[88] Indeed, the youngest son of the large family of Mellor boys, Douglas Holden Mellor, died at Higher House on the 13th December 1964, aged 70 years. He was a former general manager of Royton Spinning Co., where he worked until its closure in 1960, and a lifelong member of St. Paul's Church, Royton, where he served as organist and choirmaster from 1918 -1939 and as churchwarden from 1941 onwards. He also wrote a number of articles about Royton and St. Paul's Church.

Around 1947, and no doubt for much longer, part of Higher House was used as a day nursery for the Bee, Fir, King, Lion and Thornham cotton mill workers.[89] The day nursery only occupied part of the building and the Mellors continued to live in the bulk of the premises until Douglas died in 1964. For a few years after Douglas Mellor's death, it became the family home of the Dunkerleys[90] and was converted into a restaurant in the 1970s.

The building had a chequered career over later years and saw many alterations and extensions. As a guest house, it was possibly known as 'Strathmore,' and in later years it underwent many changes of name, particularly when it was used as a nightclub, including Tipplers and Tramtracks, and also Jo-Jo's. During this time, the exterior was painted white and pink, with black murals of Edwardian people, which along with a garish canopy and earlier extensions, served to disguise the original grace and grandeur of Higher House.

The property finally came to the end of its natural life in 2003 when it was demolished and an estate of houses built on the site. The original grounds of Higher House were quite extensive and parts had, at an earlier point, been turned into large scale car parking. By the present day the entire footprint is covered in housing. The result is a tasteful and well-appointed area, set back from the road and reflecting the modern development of Oldham. The loss of Higher House has changed the landscape of the area and the look of the junction, but is arguably an improvement, given the sad state into which this once prominent house had fallen.

But that is not the complete end of Higher House; it has not disappeared completely without a trace. There are still a number of items of furniture and other artifacts within St. Paul's Church, Royton, donated by members of the Mellor family, together with at least one stained glass memorial. Several Mellor names appear on the war memorial and the history of the church and other Royton subjects were written by Douglas Mellor. At least one descendent of the family still attends the church on a regular basis.

Orleans House, 68 Rochdale Road

Orleans cotton mill[91] was built by Joseph Rowland in 1805, the year of the Battle of Trafalgar. It was extended on many occasions and in 1846 there were four hundred hands employed there.[92] It was probably around that time that Joseph decided to erect Orleans House on an adjacent site. It was a substantially built house, mainly of two storeys with an additional attic and cellar. The house was situated at the junction of Rochdale Road and St. Mary's Way; opposite Grange School, on Rowland Street,[93] which is no longer there.

The 1861 Census lists Joseph Rowland as a 58-year-old cotton manufacturer, the son of the original founder of the mill, who bore the same name. He was living with his wife, Elizabeth, who was 55 years old; their three children Anne, aged 27; Joseph, 23; and James Brierley Rowland who was 17 years old. There were also two live-in servants employed. Although the property was also listed in street directories between that year and 1895, the 1871 Census does not specifically mention Orleans House and ten years later, in 1881, Joseph Rowland, the brother of James, is referred to as the occupier of the house. He was described as being un-married, 43 years old, a magistrate and cotton manufacturer.

Sometime between 1884 and 1888, the cotton mill ceased production and was demolished. As cotton mills went, Orleans was quite small and was probably uneconomical at the time. The 1891 Census is the first recorded instance of the property being referred to as 68, Rochdale Road as opposed to Orleans House, when the occupants listed were Joseph Rowland, aged 53, and William E. Rowland, his nephew, who was a nineteen year old learning cotton manufacturing. There were also two servants. It is thought that Joseph either died or moved away shortly after this time, because the occupier of Orleans House in 1900 is given as Joseph R. Sanderson.[94] Perhaps reflecting the fact that Orleans House was via the small road, named after its originating family, the following year's electoral roll lists the property as 102 Rowland Street. But by this time, the street name was the only link; the family having been replaced by a Watson Ireland, the District Registrar of Births and Deaths. It is assumed that Watson Ireland lived there until 1910[95] when William Fordell is described as being resident.

In the 1920s several other occupiers are listed, until eventually Orleans House, sometime around the late 1950s or early 1960s was taken over by the RSPCA as an animal clinic. This use continued right up until 1981, when the RSPCA relocated to Rhodes Bank, at which point the house became empty for a while before being used as a store for parts in connection with the newly built Nissan garage and showroom on St. Mary's Way. It was finally demolished in 1998, the site now forming part of the car parking area for the said garage.

The name of the house and mill are perpetuated by Orleans Way, part of the housing development sited to the east.

---

[86] It is assumed that the building was called Higher House because it lay, at that time, towards the higher end of Royton village. There wasn't a Lower House, as far as can be ascertained.
[87] http://www.econ.ku.dk/Research/Publications/pink/2007/0703.pdf (Accessed April 2007).
[88] Residents of Oldham may recall an exhibition on Higher House held at Royton Library in 1985.
[89] For details of what happened to these mills, please see Higher House Appendix.
[90] Very little is known about them and they only remained in residence for a very short time.
[91] Likely named because of its connection with the cotton growing areas of America.
[92] To put this in context see http://www.spartacus.schoolnet.co.uk/IRashley.htm and for other factory related statistics go to: http://links.jstor.org/sici?sici=00130133(191509)25%3A99%3C475%3ASFSO1%3E2.0.CO%3B2-A
[93] Named after its owner.
[94] Source: the Burgess Roll and also the 1901 Census.
[95] Source: the Burgess Roll.

Springbank, Grange Avenue

*Springbank, 2007.
©D. Gurr. Reproduced with the kind permission of D. Gurr.*

Before considering the history of this house, it is necessary to look first at one of its more prominent and remarkable occupiers, Alfred Butterworth.[96] He was born in 1838, the son of James Butterworth, a linen-draper of Greenacres Moor. His mother died when he was only ten months old and at the age of thirteen he became an apprentice at Platt Bros.

During the next six years Alfred gained an insight into the lives and work of the labourers, mechanics and their families, which apparently made a lasting impression on him and resulted in a lifelong empathy for the poor.

When he was nineteen years of age, Alfred joined the firm established by his father at Springfield Mill in Chadderton, namely Shaw and Butterworth. His father, having already laid the foundations of the firm, soon left the management of the mill to Alfred and Mr. Shaw.

Alfred married Mary, second daughter of Edmund Hartley, a Director of Platt Bros. in August 1862 and moved into Springbank House, a large mansion split into two dwellings,[97] standing near to the junction of Grange Avenue and Manchester Road (A62) in modern day Werneth.

The firm of Shaw and Butterworth prospered to the extent that in 1866 they moved their enterprise to the larger Glebe Mills nearby. Here, hard work and a shrewd business sense brought continued success and over the years Alfred Butterworth made himself a fortune. When Mr. Shaw retired, Alfred formed new partnerships and the firm became known as Stansfield, Butterworth and Murgatroyd.

Alfred was, to the core, a sincere Christian whose life reflected Christian principles. He was very much a law unto himself, qualities that did not always endear him to his fellow employers in the Federation of Master Cotton Spinners. He would sometimes award his operatives an extra week's wages and he also inaugurated an old age pension scheme for all employees, long before the outset of the Welfare State.

The 1871 Census is the first to record the name of Alfred Butterworth, then aged 32 years, his wife, Mary Ann, five years younger, their three children: Edith Annie, aged 7, James Hartley who was 5 and Alice two years old. They also employed two live-in servants. In the 1875 Street Directory, the address of the property is given, like so many others in the district, as Werneth Park. The occupier of the other part of the house was registered as John Seed.

Though he played a prominent part in public affairs, Alfred never stood for election to Oldham Council. He was, however, a Justice of the Peace and President of Oldham Royal Infirmary. He was a generous friend to many religious and philanthropic societies and gave £1,000 (worth something like £62,000 in today's purchasing power) towards the building of Christ Church in Chadderton; he founded and maintained medical missions in the area and was also a keen supporter of Hollinwood Working Men's Institute and President of the Town Mission.

In 1878 Alfred Butterworth purchased the Hatherden Estate,[98] comprising some 1,460 acres of Hampshire farmland, together with Hatherden House for £7,000. He never made his home there, however, preferring to travel down from Oldham by rail at weekends to liaise with the bailiff who managed the estate. Public spirited as always, Alfred became a trustee and manager of the local school; provided a reading room in the village and was largely responsible for securing a free library in the neighbouring town of Andover, which opened on the 11th July 1899 immediately after he was granted the Freedom of that Borough.

By 1881 Alfred and Mary's two eldest children had apparently left the family home, although another baby, Marian, had been born. The number of servants living in the household had been increased to four. The Census also included the names of John Watson Seed, a 49 year old cotton spinner; his wife, Betsy, aged 43; four children; and three servants. Some time prior to 1888 John W. Seed must have died, because by the 1891 Census, Betsy is described as the 'head of the household,' a 53 year old widow, with her eleven year old daughter, Hilda, and three servants. At the time of the 1901 Census, the Butterworth family had been joined at Springbank by Harold Wrigley and his family. By this time, Alfred was described as being 62 years old, whilst Mary Ann was 57. No other members of their family were living at home and only two servants remained at the house.

On Friday 17th January 1913, shortly after celebrating his golden wedding anniversary, Alfred paid his last visit to Glebe Mills. Six days later he died peacefully at Springbank and was buried on the 27th of that month in Chadderton Cemetery. In Christ Church, Chadderton, the great west stained glass window was dedicated in 1871; the year after the church was built, in memory of Edmund and Ann Hartley, the parents of Alfred Butterworth's wife, Mary Ann. Another stained glass window in the church was given in memory of Alfred by his widow in October 1913, shortly before her own death.

The west stained glass window at Christ Church, Chadderton, 2007.
©D. Gurr. Reproduced with the kind permission of D. Gurr.

Sometime prior to 1918, the house was re-named Westlands and the Street Directory for that year gives the occupiers as James and Prockter Stott. In 1924 the house was occupied by Albert Cooper and William Smith Stott, but by 1934 Albert Houghton and Helena Stott were in residence there, between them employing four servants.

The building was purchased by the Local Authority in 1948, linked back together again and converted into a home for the aged two years later. During the 1970s it housed the 'Talking Newspaper', a publication for people with visual impairments.[99]

The home closed down towards the end of 1993 and for a while was used as offices. The building was later occupied for children's education, but is currently vacant. The building will, no doubt, serve the people of Oldham again, probably as a care home or of some other similar purpose.

[96] Follow this link for interesting information of Mitchell and Kenyon film of Alfred Butterworth. http://www.imdb.com/title/tt0471071/ (Accessed April 2007).

[97] This split may well have occurred around 1850. The reason for splitting into two separate dwellings was probably straightforward economics and seemed to apply to a number of houses in the area.

[98] Visit this website for more information on Hatherden Estate. http://www.hants.gov.uk/tangleyparish/misc/bookpage.html

[99] The talking Newspaper still exists, but has moved on at least two other occasions.

Sunnyside House

Despite having a number of gaps in its history, the parts we can piece together are well-documented and make Sunnyside House a worthwhile inclusion in this book. John Murgatroyd, a partner in the cotton firm of Butterworth and Murgatroyd[100] built Sunnyside House towards the end of Chamber Road (off Manchester Road, A62) sometime between 1871 and 1875. Prior to that, he had lived at 217, Manchester Road, Hollinwood.

Nathaniel Littler, a partner in the cotton spinning concern of Prockter, Littler & Co. was also listed as being in occupation there in 1875, and as you will have noted from other houses in this book, this is likely to be the case when a large house has been split into separate dwellings.

The 1881 Census states that John Murgatroyd was aged 45 years and his wife, Ellen, was 39. They had five children between the ages of three and ten years and one servant. The whole family was still together and in situ in 1891, as recorded by the Census. Nathaniel Littler, however, had by this time died, because the Littler portion of the property was now headed by his widow, Ellen, aged 78 years. Three of her young grandchildren were living with her, together with one servant.

By the time of the next Census in 1901, there is no mention of either John or Ellen Murgatroyd and it is assumed that they may have both died in the interim period. The 'head of the household' was now Arnold Murgatroyd, eldest son of John and Ellen and aged twenty-nine. He was single and one of his sisters and two brothers were also living at Sunnyside House, this co-existence of siblings in the family home epitomized the times and was common to many households. Ellen Littler was also still living there, although her age of 80 appeared to have been recorded wrongly, either at the previous Census or this one. A grandson and two servants were living with her.

The Murgatroyd family built the Royd cotton mill alongside Sunnyside House in 1907 and soon afterwards formed the Royd Mill Ltd. to run the business. They remained at Sunnyside House until at least 1918 and possibly longer, although they are thought to have sold the firm in the early 1920s, subsequently moving to Conway in north Wales.

The Burgess Rolls for the years 1927, 1934 and 1938, all list a number of different occupiers, including the Bridge family. This might suggest that the house was now divided up even further, into several apartments.

What is known is that the Lancashire Cotton Corporation took over Royd Mill in the 1930s and after the Second World War, they used Sunnyside House for a time as a central testing and research centre for new types of cotton fabric. This use continued until 1958 when the firm, later part of Courtaulds, moved these operations to Thornycroft on Newport Street (see separate entry). Sunnyside House was sold in 1964 to the then newly-formed Polish Association, who converted it into a flourishing social club, a use that continues until the present day.

The last surviving male member of the prominent Murgatroyd family of Oldham was Nathaniel, the son of John and Ellen, who died on the 15th January 1964 aged 88 years. His elder brothers, Dr. Alfred and Mr. Arnold Murgatroyd, had together managed the spinning business and there were also two sisters and two nieces, one of whom was married to the actor, Jack Howarth. Jack Howarth is probably best remembered and loved by people the world over as the character Albert Tatlock whom he played for many years in the Granada Television programme, Coronation Street.

Royd Mill ceased production of cotton in 1981. The cheerfully named Sunnyside House is one of those that has withstood the ravages of time. It is still standing and in common with all the other mill houses in this book, which have survived into the 21st Century, is well worth the effort of visiting, even if one can only view the outside. Royd Mill is currently occupied by a firm of textile factors.

Thornycroft, Newport Street

Thornycroft, 2007.
©*D. Gurr. Reproduced with the kind permission of D. Gurr.*

Amongst the most recent of our historical houses, it is thought that Thornycroft, on Newport Street (adjacent to Frederick Street and in the vicinity of Manchester Road A62 on the Coppice) was built around 1872. Edward Wright Wrigley and his wife, Mary, moved to Thornycroft in 1880. He was a 43 year old cotton spinner and in the partnership of Lees and Wrigley of Greenbank Mills, Glodwick.[101] Residing with him was his wife, Mary, aged 37. They employed three servants who lived in the house. The stained glass windows in the entrance hall still incorporate the letter 'W' in the design, as can be seen from the photograph on the following page. Edward and Mary had three sons living with them: Arthur Edward, born 1865; Harold, born 1866; and Vincent Shiers, 1867; however, the 1881 Census makes no mention of these children and it is assumed that all three were away at boarding school when data was collected.

It is interesting to note that both this Census and the 1880 Street Directory list Thornycroft as being on Wellington Road, whereas, by 1888 it was listed under Frederick Street. As is sometimes the case when comparing historical information across a number of sources, a common conflict of information occurs when the 1891 Census, unlike the Street Directory, still listed the property under Wellington Road. Harold, by this time aged 24, and his brother, Vincent, a year younger, were both described as cotton spinners and the number of servants living in had increased to five.

Edward Wrigley died on March 8th 1900, aged 68 years and was survived by his wife and four sons, who all became directors of the firm. In addition to Harold and Vincent mentioned above, were Arthur and Edward Whittaker Wrigley. His widow and sons placed a stained glass window in memory of Edward Wright Wrigley in St. Mark's Church at Glodwick and a marble tablet was also raised there by the workpeople of Greenbank Mills.

By 1901, the Census confirms that only Mary, aged sixty-three and Arthur who was thirty-six, were resident at the house, although Arthur married later in the year and then moved to Woodfield.[102] Mary, in fact, continued to live there until her own death on the 8th April 1919, aged 81 years. Edward Whittaker Wrigley later became chairman of the company and died at Ganton Hall,[103] Scarborough, in the North Riding of Yorkshire, on the 13th November 1965, aged 72 years. He left a nett estate of £180,480 (a purchasing power in today's terms of about £2,411,000) and his descendents still live there. Arthur, Edward's son, of similar name, was killed in action in 1942.

[100] See chapter on Springbank, Grange Avenue.
[101] See Sunnyside House and Abbeyhills House.
[102] See chapter on Woodfield.

After Mary's death, the premises then passed to Robert and Isabella McLud, who were still there in 1927 and possibly for a longer period. By 1934, however, Madge Mellowdew[104] of the Moorside cotton mill family was in occupation. Together with her sister, Irene Mary,

This stained glass window bears the Wrigley family initials and can be seen at the porch entrance.
©Nick Wrigley. Reproduced with the kind permission of Nick Wrigley.

she successfully ran a private preparatory school in Thornycroft, mainly for the children of the wealthier gentry of Oldham. In 1956 Madge Mellowdew is still listed as one of the occupiers of Thornycroft House, which appears to have been sub-divided at some time, the others being Robert Hasty and Norman Connor. We do know that a Mrs. Alice Maud Mellowdew, widow of James A. Mellowdew of Moorside, died intestate at her home in Dunham Massey, near Altrincham on the 21st of December 1963, aged eighty-four years. What is not known is whether she and 'Madge' were one and the same person. Regardless, the estate of Alice Maud was £36,371 nett or £526,000 in modern buying power.

In any event, the building was sold, approximately two years later, to the Lancashire Cotton Corporation (LCC) for use as a Central Testing and Research Centre.[105] When Courtaulds took over the LCC in 1965, they commenced a substantial re-organisation process and part of this operation involved moving the Testing Centre from Thornycroft to the top floor of nearby Heron Mill[106]. Thornycroft was then put on the market again, at a somewhat difficult time for this type and size of property, but it was eventually sold on December 12th 1968 to Oldham's prestigious Hulme Grammar School[107] for a bargain price of £11,000 (a purchasing power in today's terms of about £132,000). The school subsequently converted the premises into an annexe for their arts and crafts department, a use that continues to the present day.

The grounds of the house were always quite extensive and consisted, at one time, of a separate cottage with stables and carriage garage; three brick-built dog kennels complete with their own exercise area; a grass tennis court; a squash court (reputed to be the first privately-built one in Britain) and even a pets' graveyard. Today, although nothing of these other structures stands, Thornycroft continues to play a significant role in the life of Oldham; a continuing legacy of the Wrigley family.

Woodfield

Woodfield, c. 1910.

Woodfield was built on land belonging to the Werneth Park Estate, off Manchester Road A62, sometime prior to 1841. The Census for that year stated that the occupier and, almost certainly, the builder of the house was Andrew Schofield, a timber merchant, who was living there with his wife, Eliza, their three children: Kate, aged 7; Mary, 4; and Charles who was two, and three servants. Andrew and Eliza were both aged forty years. The family grew in the intervening

103 A quick search of the Internet reveals many sites that can be used to reference this area, and gain a feeling for the properties of this period in the North Riding. Some of them reference Killerby Old Hall, Raven Hall and the remarkably named Bogg Hall! Most references to Ganton Hall are with regard to current business use and golfing fixtures, although this site www.ryedale.gov.uk/PDF/Sherburn%2016.pdf does give some interesting historical information.
104 http://www.ancestry.com/learn/facts/Fact.aspx?fid=6&yr=1891&ln=Mellowdew

105 See chapter on Sunnyside House.
106 Designed by Sydney Stott and built in 1905. Taken over by Lancashire County Council in the 1930s. Ceased production in 1960. Occupied by Courtaulds as offices and warehouses until 1994, now a distribution warehouse for D. Jacobson and Sons Ltd., footwear importers. For other snippets of information on the Internet, try http://mancunian1001.wordpress.com/2006/11/21/oldham-wakes-uncovered/ - Stuart Vallentine's interesting and witty blog. (Accessed April 2007).
107 www.hulme-grammar.oldham.sch.uk/allschools/index.php (Accessed April 2007).

decade and, in 1851, had been supplemented by an elder son, John A.,[108] twenty years old and also a timber merchant and an additional daughter, Harriett, who was eight. The Schofield family remained at the property until the early 1860s, when it is assumed that Andrew Schofield retired and the family moved on – though we have no records of where to.

The 1871 Census lists the occupier of Woodfield as Thomas Evans Lees, a partner in the giant Glodwick cotton mill concern of Lees and Wrigley,[109] who was later to become the benefactor of St. Mark's Church at the top of Waterloo Street, adjacent to Glodwick Road, B6194. Thomas Lees was forty-one years old at that time and a magistrate. His wife, daughter and five servants were also living with him at Woodfield, but we do not have much additional information on them, only that T. E. Lees' wife was 29 years old at the time and that his daughter was called Bernarda and aged one. Despite so little detail, we do know that they did not live there more than a decade and, by 1880, the Street Directory indicates a change in ownership. Although it lists William Green and William Parry as the occupiers of Woodfield, this fact is not borne out by the following year's Census information. The Census only refers to Elizabeth Mary Bettinson, the 51 year old widowed housekeeper and was otherwise vacant at the time of the Census. Her term of occupancy was relatively short, and we know that soon afterwards, another well-known Glodwick cotton mill owner, Edward Collinge moved to the building for a short while, prior to his early death in 1890. The 1891 Census refers to Edward's widow, Emma, who was only 43 years old herself, living at the premises with her five children: Robert who was 16 years old; Wharton, 12; Ellen, 10; Mari Anne, 9; and Arthur who was 7. In common with previous occupants and giving us an idea of the scale of the building, Emma had six servants living-in at Woodfield. Records indicate that Emma and her family remained at Woodfield for the next few years, until the occupancy of Woodfield became somewhat more noteworthy on a national level.

For a short period around the turn of the 20th Century, Woodfield had arguably its most famous occupant, namely Alfred Emmott.[110] Born in Chadderton in 1858 of a prominent Quaker family, Alfred was educated firstly at a Quaker school in Kendal, moving from there to London. He was elected to Oldham Council in 1883, serving for twelve years during which time he was appointed Mayor in 1891-2. In 1899 he successfully defeated Winston Churchill to become one of Oldham's two Members of Parliament. He was made Deputy Speaker of the House of Commons in 1906 and, five years later, was raised to the peerage becoming Baron Emmott of Oldham.

Alfred Emmott had become a partner in his father's cotton business of Emmott and Walshaw at the age of twenty-three years; married Mary Gertrude Lees in 1887; and rose to become Chairman of Platt Bros[111] and director of several other companies. He served a total of 43 years on Oldham Chamber of Commerce and was also a Justice of the Peace. When visiting the town in December 1926, Lord Emmott appeared to be in the picture of good health, but within a few days of returning to his London home, he died suddenly of a heart attack at the age of 68 years. Having no male heir, his title expired with his death.

Woodfield was also vacant at the time of the 1901 Census; but this was to be a significant period for the house. Later in the year, upon his marriage, the building was occupied by Arthur E. Wrigley, a partner of the Lees and Wrigley cotton empire at Greenbank Mills, Glodwick. Mr. Wrigley, a former Conservative candidate for Oldham, laid the foundation stone for the 'new' Conservative Club on Union Street in 1911, which replaced a former club that had been built on the same site in 1874.[112] This stone is still clearly visible adjacent to the front doors of the building, even though the use of the property has changed. The premises were used as a nightclub for a time; appropriately named "Mr. Wrigley's." Arthur Wrigley left Oldham in 1936 and died in 1952, at the age of 87 years.

By 1915 Emma Fletcher was listed as living at Woodfield, but around 1927 the premises were sold and converted into a private maternity home. Details are patchy, but it is likely that the maternity home was absorbed into the National Health Service. It is clear, however, that it continued up to and beyond 1979. The building is currently used as a nursery for children with severe disabilities.

It is worth making the effort to visit Woodfield to examine the exterior, as it retains many of the Victorian architectural features that characterise important dwellings of the time. Create a mental bubble around yourself, filter out the noise of modern day traffic and immerse yourself in Woodfield's frontage, which speaks volumes about the achievements, hopes and aspirations of our recent Oldham ancestors. But perhaps most of all, having read this book, take time to look at modern Oldham and how it has built itself upon the roots of our industrial past – it too has aspirations and hopes every bit as strong as our Georgian and Victorian predecessors. What we leave to future generations will be every bit as revealing as the fascinating histories of our mill houses of Oldham.

[108] Who is not mentioned in 1841.
[109] See also the chapter on Abbeyhills House.
[110] For further information: http://en.wikipedia.org/wiki/Alfred_Emmott,_1st_Baron_Emmott
[111] There are a wide number of reference points for Platt Brothers. Suggestions include the Oldham Local Studies and Archives:
  http://www.oldham.gov.uk/community/local_studies
  http://en.wikipedia.org/wiki/Oldham
  The National Archives: http://www.nationalarchives.gov.uk/nra/searches/codocs.asp?CR=B6437
  You might also like to visit Dobcross. Bridge House at the junction with Sugar Lane and Nicker Brow has a blue plaque commemorating the significant contribution of this company to local and world trade.
[112] Presently unoccupied and almost opposite the Oldham Chronicle Building on Union Street.

Appendices

Appendix : Crompton House / Hall

The first reference to the Crompton family was in 1442, when a lease was renewed between Henry de Merland, Vicar of Rochdale and John de Crompton. This related to the Crompton Hall Estate and Shore Edge (now Buckstones Road). The original deed was for one messuage (i.e. dwelling house, outbuildings and land) at the rent of forty shillings yearly, plus two hens and two capons, to be paid at the Feast of the Nativity. A later occupier was Thomas de Crompton, probably John's son and his family.

This hall is thought to have been a typical mediaeval building, with a central hall open to the rafters and probably a two-storey section at each end. When Thomas de Crompton died in 1608, the estate passed to his three daughters. Later occupiers included Hugh and Alice Yannis in 1642. Hugh was a wealthy landowner who gave land near Lees for the building of Hey Chapel, now St. John's, Hey, and also conveyed the Whetstone Hill Estate to a certain John Kershaw; William Richardson who paid taxes for two hearths in 1666; and Isaac and Joseph Jackson who conveyed two-thirds of the estate to John Kershaw in 1755. It was demolished around 1848, after the Milne family, another large cotton mill family, purchased the land.

The hall was later re-built, incorporating some of the 15th Century oak panelling and a magnificent open fireplace. However, it also included an improbable Scots baronial tower and other Victorian extravagances. Members of the Milne family still resided at the 'new' hall until at least 1905. In 1950, Mr. Edward Leigh, the then owner of Crompton Hall, sold the premises to a demolition firm and it was pulled down in March 1952. A bungalow now stands on the site of the hall on Buckstones Road, with other housing planned for the grounds.

Appendix: Crossbank House, Lees

A far as can be determined, Hey is another word for an enclosed space, as in pastureland or common. The name appears in the description of Birch Hall, i.e. Rhodes Hey, Middle Rhodes Hey and Further Rhodes Hey, all near Rhodes Hill. There was a Further Hey cotton mill situated near to St. John's Church, Hey, built prior to 1844 and occupied in 1852 by Isaac and Samuel Seville, who always wore silk hats and drove to business in a four wheeled dog cart.

Whether they belong to the same family as the Crossbank Sevilles is not known, because it was a common name in the neighbourhood – but it was close by and Isaac is common to both. The mill ceased production in 1939 and was used as a barracks during the Second World War. It was destroyed by fire on the 31st October 1958 and the site has been used for housing since 1971. Heyside in Royton may have the same derivation.

One further link between the names Crossbank and Hey lies in the fact that near to Further Hey Cotton Mill, in the River Medlock Valley, there was also situated Cross Bank Sewage Works, an undertaking belonging to Limehurst Rural District Council.

Appendix: Higher House

With reference to the mills cited in the Higher House chapter, you might be interested in the following:

Bee Mill, Shaw Road. Ceased spinning in 1964. Was purchased by the Local Authority in 1985 and the top two storeys demolished. Slumberland Ltd. occupied the remainder.

Fir Mill, Highbarn Road. Ceased spinning in 1959 and was later used by catering equipment engineers until 1996.

King Mill, Shaw Road. Ceased spinning in 1959. Demolished in 1982.

Lion Mill, Fitton Street. Ceased spinning 1967. Re-occupied 1969 by Wellcome Foundation Ltd.

Thornham Mill, Oozewood Road. Two mills ceased production in 1962. One was demolished and the other is likely to be demolished shortly.

Appendix: The British Census

The collection of data relating to the population of a country can be found through history.[113] The Romans certainly took a Census, as is mentioned in The Bible, and William The Conqueror's Domesday Book is certainly a Census of sorts. Some readers will be familiar with the modern British Census, which was inaugurated on a limited basis in 1801.[114] By 1841[115] a more structured Census, which detailed occupants as well as property and land, was in place. In all its forms, the chief function was, and remains:
• To register the individuals resident in each area of the British Isles;
• To record their occupations;
• To list their dwellings and associated land ownership;
• Increasingly, to act as a repository of accumulating knowledge about the lifestyle and choices of the variety and diversity of people that make up the population, all for the purpose of calculating national wealth and trends in population growth and migration. This data is, in turn, used to form decisions made on how the wealth of the nation is spent and where there are gaps in provision of services.
Much of what we know about the 20 houses listed here is drawn from this collection of information, from 1801 to the present day. Over the years, the Census has changed to collect the type of data presented by an increasingly diverse population. Today, for instance, the Census requires us to reveal information about:
• Gender
• Income
• Religion
However, a Census can only tell us so much, and in fact, as evidence will show, sometimes it can show us nothing at all! Complementing this extensive record is the Burgess Roll – see separate appendix.

Appendix: The Burgess Roll

In 1832 parliament underwent a series of reforms regarding eligibility to vote. This was followed, in 1835, by that of the constitution of municipal corporations, or in other words, the formation of administrative boroughs, which included the creation of a uniform qualification now known as the old Burgess qualification.[116] This meant one had to be registered in an area to vote.

The meaning of the term Burgess comes from an early word for an inhabitant of a borough:[117]
"BURGESS (Med. Lat. burgensis, from burgus, a borough, a town), a term, in its earliest sense, meaning an inhabitant of a borough, one who occupied a tenement therein, but now applied solely to a registered parliamentary, or more strictly, municipal voter. An early use of the word was to denote a member elected to parliament by his fellow citizens in a borough. In some of the American colonies (e.g. Virginia), a "burgess" was a member of the legislative body, which was termed the "House of Burgesses." Previous to the Municipal Reform Act 1835, burgess was an official title in some English boroughs, and in this sense is still used in some of the states of the United States, as in Connecticut, New Jersey, Pennsylvania. The Burgessroll is the register or official list of burgesses in a borough."

Oldham Local Studies and Archives library holds a full set of Burgess Roll and electoral registers going back to 1850 but the complete run covers the town of Oldham only. There are gaps during both world wars, when registers were not published and many unexplained anomalies where houses and/or individual occupiers do not always appear.

Coverage of surrounding districts is not as good and there are many gaps, for instance Royton is covered 1851, 1871 - 1915 and 1973 only. The Lancashire Record Office in Preston holds registers from 1934 - 1946 but it is an incomplete run.[118]

Appendix: Oral Tradition

One of the most important cultural sources of information remains the oral tradition; the tales and details handed down to us from people who actually knew the houses and occupants involved. No other record can capture the depth of detail as that of the stories told to us by our parents and grandparents. They colour them with the minutiae of the time and link them up so that each place and event relates with others around, to give us a more complete picture of the time. With this information we can understand more easily why decisions were made and what motivated people to live in certain ways and undertake certain activities. The oral tradition can cascade down through many generations, as stories of particular note and worth are repeated from parent to child, so that we can have a direct oral link between a modern day Oldham child and his ancestor of 100 years or more.

The furthest back in time that we have been able to gather information is the 13th Century, in the case of Crompton House. Documents of this age are scarce and oral tradition non existent, but there survive tantalising glimpses of the area in this dim and distant time, through individual documents relating to the surrounding area. However, most of the histories in this book draw from 1801 and forward. They are not fully comprehensive – gaps in records and simply the fact that research is an ongoing process mean that there is still plenty to learn about the area now designated Oldham Borough.

It is hoped that the gaps will intrigue you as much as the information and, possibly, even inspire you to undertake your own research or offer up any evidence you might have in your family to make the picture more complete.

Appendix: Social Status

The Census shows us who the occupiers are, but does not necessarily determine their status. An occupier can be a landowner, a property owner, or possibly a tenant. This lack of detail can often lead to confusion and is a feature of some of the uncertainty we have about the relationships between people living at the same address.

The hierarchy of the English class system was very much in evidence during the lives of these houses, pretty much up until the 1960s, when many social and economic factors amalgamated to change the face of Britain as a whole. Whilst the current parliament debates, as it has done for the past 80 years, the fate of the House of Lords, the role of minor aristocracy is evident in some of the houses portrayed in this book. However, equally as interesting is the fact that the bulk of the properties were actually the result of new money gained through the Industrial Revolutions, rather than inherited old money. The aristocratically owned Clarksfield Estate may have been the base on which new mill house owners built, but it was the money generated from the mills themselves that allowed the building of Lower and Higher Clarksfield Houses.

Titles are evident in the history of our houses, but they do not abound and most are of the more lowly stature. For instance, the title of Baronet[119] (abbreviated to Bart. or Bt.) denotes a member of the British order of honour, which ranks below a Baron but above a Knight. It is a hereditary title and, originally, denoted an English Baron who had lost the right of their individual summons to parliament. Baronets were and are addressed by the prefix Sir rather than Lord.

At the other end of the social scale was a Chapman. The Oxford Dictionary defines a Chapman as a peddler – someone who travels around selling his or her wares. One occupant of Copster House was described in this way. In fact, Copster House seems to have housed people from a variety of social standings, as one of its owners is identified as a Yeoman. This term seems to have had many meanings over the years, including a ceremonial officer guarding a monarch, a servant in the royal household and freeholder or farmer of a smallholding. It is currently a division of the British Army[120]. However, wherever it is used in this book, it is always in the context of the person being referred to as a freeholder or farmer.

There are many terms allocated to people who worked within the cotton and wool industries.[121] For instance, cotton doubler, piecer,[122] spinner, stripper, grinder and weaver[123] and carder[124] and each of whom held their own status within the industry and were paid accordingly.[125]

Social structure in Georgian and Victorian Britain is a well-documented topic, which cannot be done justice to in such a small space as this, but it is hoped that the links provided will give you a good starting point to explore the subject further and gain a deeper understanding of the roles and rules of industrial life during the early days of our houses.

Appendix: Directories

Readers will be familiar with telephone directories, which we use to locate businesses and residents of each town and city. Over the years many different forms of directories have been employed, many purely for commercial purposes and some, as in the case of the more recent Diocese of Manchester Street Directory,[126] for general public information. Many are regional, such as Worrall's Street Directories of Oldham, and historians are invariably indebted to the Kelly's Directories of the past.[127]

If your ancestors were in business in Oldham they may appear in a variety of Trade Directories. Oldham Local Studies and Archives hold local directories dating from 1814. These Directories vary in content, listing by trade, address or surname. The Directories can be particularly useful for locating addresses when trying to trace a family in the Census.

Oldham Local Studies and Archives also hold telephone directories for the Oldham area for the following years:
1923, 1963, 1967, 1968, 1970, 1972, 1975, 1977, 1982, 1985, 1986, 1988, 1989, 1991, 1993, 1996, 1999, 2000.

[113] http://www.lib.unc.edu/reference/govinfo/census/documentation.html
[114] http://www.british-genealogy.com/resources/census/index.htm
[115] http://en.wikipedia.org/wiki/UK_Census
[116] For this and more on registration and its role in governance and census, visit: http://www.1911encyclopedia.org/Registration
[117] The definition appears on the Love To Know website: http://www.1911encyclopedia.org/Burgess (Accessed May 2007).
[118] http://www.genuki.org.uk/big/eng/LAN/Oldham/
[119] http://www.google.com/search?hl=en&rlz=1T4SUNA_en___GB203&defl=en&q=define:baronet&sa=X&oi=glossary_definition&ct=title
[120] http://www.army.mod.uk/royalyeomanry/index.htm (Accessed May 2007).
[121] For a well presented website on the history of just one Cotton Mill in Lancashire: http://www.ourwardfamily.com/cotton_trade.htm and http://www.aboutlancs.com/cotton.htm (Accessed May 2007).
[122] For further reference to the work of young children in cotton mills, try http://www.scotsfamily.com/occupations.htm and, http://www.cottontimes.co.uk/wheelgateo.htm and http://www.spartacus.schoolnet.co.uk/IRpiecers.htm (Accessed May 2007).
[123] For definitions of some of these terms, visit: http://www.ourwardfamily.com/cotton_trade.htm#Cotton%20Mill%20Workers (Accessed May 2007).
[124] http://en.wikipedia.org/wiki/Carding (Accessed May 2007).
[125] For some excellent general information on the wool and cotton industries in Oldham and Manchester, I would recommend: http://www.spartacus.schoolnet.co.uk/TEXcotton.htm (Accessed May 2007)
[126] http://www.manchester.anglican.org/churches.asp?DeaneryCode=22
Kellys was a hard back directory published in many major towns. Now it can be accessed at: http://www.kellysearch.co.uk/

Bibliography

Other sources you may like to access, many of which were used in the research and writing of this book.

Bains and Butterworth - http://www.lancs.ac.uk/depts/history/research/baines.htm

Bateson, Hartley
A Centenary History of Oldham (Oldham Council, 1949)

Butterworth, Edwin
The History of Ashton-Under-Lyne (W. D. Varey, Manchester,1842)

Butterworth, Edwin
Historical Sketches of Oldham (E. J. Morten, 1856)

Gurr, Duncan
The Dronsfield Story, 1992 (available at browse at Oldham Local Studies and Archives).

Gurr, Duncan & Julian Hunt
The Cotton Mills of Oldham 3rd Edition (Oldham Arts & Heritage Publications, Oldham MBC, 1998)

Hunt, Julian & Frances Stott
Looking Back at Crompton (Oldham Arts & Heritage Publications, Oldham MBC, 1988)

Lawson, Michael & Mark Johnson
Looking Back at Chadderton (Oldham Arts & Heritage Publications, Oldham MBC, 1990)

Magee, Rob
A History of Crompton and Shaw Pubs (Neil Richardson, 1988)

Magee, Rob
Inns and Alehouses of Oldham and their licensees 1714-1992 (Neil Richardson, 1992)

Magee, Rob
The Oldham Beerhouses and their licensees 1828-1994 Part One (Neil Richardson, 1994)

Magee, Rob
The Oldham Beerhouses and their licensees 1828-1994 Part Two (Neil Richardson, 1994)

Magee, Rob
Failsworth Pubs 1731-1995 and their licensees (Neil Richardson, 1995)

Magee, Rob
Springhead and Lees pubs, inc. Alt with their licensees 1717-1996 (Neil Richardson, 1996)

Magee, Rob
Saddleworth Pubs and their licensees c.1674-1998 (Neil Richardson, 1998)

Magee, Rob
Chadderton Pubs and their licensees 1750-1999 (Neil Richardson, 1999)

Moses, Roy
Going, Going, Gone (Oldham Arts & Heritage Publications, Oldham MBC, 1990)

Peat, Alan
The Rowbottom Diaries – 1781-1799 (Oldham Arts & Heritage Publications, Oldham MBC, 1996)

Saddleworth Historical Society
Various Saddleworth Bulletins.

Shaw, Giles
The Annals of Oldham (Oldham Standard, 1910)

Stott, Frances
Looking Back at Royton (Oldham Arts & Heritage Publications, Oldham MBC, 1994)

Stott, Frances
The Changing Face of Crompton (Oldham Arts & Heritage Publications, Oldham MBC, 1996)

Stott, Frances
A History of Royton Hall (Greenfield House Publications, 2001)

Taylor, Jane
Frozen Music (Oldham MBC, 1975)

Taylor, Sheila
Failsworth Place and People, (Oldham Arts & Heritage Publications, Oldham MBC, 2001)

Yates, S. W. (Ed.)
The Oldham Co-operative Record 1908-1912 (Oldham Industrial Co-operative Society)

Census Returns 1841-1901

Obituary Notices

Newspaper Articles

Burgess Rolls

Street and Trade Directories